Christian A. Schwarz / Chr...

IMPLEMENTATION GUIDE TO NATU... P9-DGQ-803

ChurchSmart
RESOURCES

St. Charles, IL 60174
1-800-253-4276

Published by ChurchSmart Resources

We are an evangelical Christian publisher committed to producing excellent products at affordable prices to help church leaders accomplish effective ministry in the areas of church planting, church growth, church renewal and leadership development.

For a free catalog of our resources call 1-800-253-4276.

Cover design by: Julie Becker
Manuscript edited by: Edward Rowell

ISBN 1-889638-03-X

Natural Church Development

Christian A. Schwarz • Christoph Schalk

The foundational introduction to Natural Church Development:

Christian A. Schwarz

Natural Church Development

Hardcover, 128 pages, illustrated in four colors throughout, with over 100 four-color photos and graphics.

ISBN 1-889638-00-5

Retail price $19.95 in U.S. dollars.

In 1998, Natural Church Development will be available in 24 different languages and in 45 countries. All foreign language edition titles and addresses of distributors can found on our website: http://www.CundP.de/international

Contents

What You Can Expect From This Book...And What You Should Not Expect

This workbook helps interested Christians implement the principles previously described in *Natural Church Development* in their own church. It starts where the previous book ended, and stops where the other practical resources for all eight quality characteristics begin.

"This book is for Christians and churches who ask themselves: How does this work practically?"

- It does *not* attempt to win anyone over to support natural church development, nor does it attempt to persuade the skeptic.

- It does *not* present the foundations of natural church development. Those are developed in the previous book *Natural Church Development*.

- It does *not* treat the theological framework on which this approach to church growth builds. The German book *Paradigmenwechsel in der Kirche* (Paradigm Shift in the Church) is dedicated to this question.

- It does *not* attempt to entertain, it does *not* pretend to be pleasant reading. It is consciously written as a pure workbook.

The Function of this Book in the Total System

Natural church development is based on the most comprehensive research project ever conducted on the causes of church growth—more than 1000 churches in 32 countries on all 5 continents were studied. This book does not present the research findings. Rather, it attempts to put the most important results of this study into practical use in your own church.

What Is Assumed

This book assumes a basic understanding of the building blocks and vocabulary of natural church development. "Growth automatisms," "Eight quality characteristics," "Biotic principles," "Spiritualizing and Technocratic Paradigms," "Principle-oriented versus Model-oriented approach," "Minimum strategy," "The 65-hypothesis,"—these are just a few examples of the terminology that will not be explained in detail in this book. What you will find are short definition boxes with references to the previous book *Natural Church Development* (abbreviated NCD), placed on crucial pages where the relevance and application of these terms to your church are discussed. An example for such a definition box you see on this page with the explanation for the term "natural church development."

Double Function

This book has a double function:

- First, it is an implementation guide for the principles of natural church development. For this reason it will certainly be used also by churches that are not yet developing a church profile.

- Second, it is the companion volume for any church that wants to do a church profile. It summarizes the practical suggestions referred to by the computer analysis.

> *Natural church development aims to release the potential that God has already put into your church.* See NCD, pages 6-14

The non-narrative style, use of tables, worksheets, checklists, and finally the use of computers in the context of conducting a church profile, may strike some readers as technocratic. For this reason we might comment here that natural church development has little in common with technocratic thinking, that is, the illusion that the church could ever be "made" to grow through human energy. Rather, it views itself as an alternative paradigm of church growth.

The Goal: to Develop the Individuality of Your Church

We realize this introduction has almost turned into a "warning." If you want to read on—or better: to continue to work—you must be quite motivated. But if you choose to come along with us through the next chapters, you will develop a greater sensitivity for the personality of your church. You will no longer search for standard recipes or successful model churches to be imitated. Rather, you will want to invest all your energy in developing the potential which God has already placed in your church.

Is this something simple? No, it is a rather difficult path. Will the rest of Christianity applaud in awe? No, you can assume probably the contrary. Is it worth it? Yes, absolutely.

Fall 1997   Christian Schwarz / Christoph Schalk

How to Develop Your Church Profile

Effective therapy depends on an accurate diagnosis. There is no wonder pill that helps every "patient." What is just right for one, turns out to be wrong for another. In Natural Church Development, the church survey is the key to getting an accurate diagnosis. This section explains why it is necessary for diagnosis, then how to accurately survey your church.

Why Develop a Church Profile?

*"Without diag-
nosis you run
into the danger
to prescribe
glasses for
short-sighted-
ness when the
problem is
cataracts."*

Do you have a small garden around your house? Then maybe you have already tried to raise your own vegetables. Do you remember the work necessary to raise a great harvest of juicy red tomatoes?

During springtime, you probably planted the young tomato plants. Perhaps you even grew them yourself from seeds. As the plants grew, each of them needed support, so you tied them up. Then you made sure that the plants had enough water and fertilizer. In the beginning, you may even have had to protect the tomato plants from those frosty nights. If your plants were growing in a greenhouse, you had to make sure that the heater was on for the night.

What does all this have to do with natural church development or its practical implementation?

Think about it: When do you water your tomato plants? When do you use fertilizer? When do you turn on the greenhouse heater? Do you water when the weatherman has forecast frost? Do you fertilize when the ground is dry and hard? No, you select the right time to do the right thing—you water when it is dry, and you provide protection when there is frost predicted. To know what that "right thing" is, you constantly conduct your own "analysis": perhaps a check of the soil with your thumb to see how dry it really is. You check the barometer regularly and keep informed about the weather. An advanced gardener may even conduct a real soil analysis to check the soil's nutrient content scientifically. These "surveys" provide you with the information necessary to decide what your tomatoes need most and when they need it.

The church profile indicates how well developed each of the quality characteristics of growing churches are in your situation and what your present minimum factor is.

That is how we recommend you proceed when you approach the practical steps of natural church development. Instead of wild, impromptu gardening, that is, attempting to build a church on the spur of the moment without coordination, you begin by asking: what is the decisive key factor at this moment for the development of my church?

**First the
Diagnosis, Then
the Therapy**

Imagine you have an appointment with your optometrist because lately you have had difficulty in reading small print. When you get there, instead of carefully diagnosing your problem, your optometrist hands you one of his own pairs of glasses and says: "Some time ago, I had the same kind of problem. These glasses really helped me. Take them with you. They will surely help you."

Would you trust this optometrist? Surely not, yet scenes like this are common in the world of church growth. Isn't it astonishing how often people "prescribe" recipes and well-meant counsel without having spent any time diagnosing the real problem? "A church in Chicago now has its worship service on Wednesday evening, and since then, everything has gone better. You should try what they have done." "What you need are skits during the worship service." "What you really need is a prayer summit—then your city will be converted." "In Argentina, they solve all their problems through spiritual warfare—you should also give it a try."

Natural church development avoids this mistaken approach and intentionally starts with the diagnosis step. The reason why we did the international research in the last year was first of all to develop a reliable diagnostic tool for local churches. To be sure, diagnosis is not everything, but without it there is—metaphysically speaking—the danger of offering a prescription for shortsightedness to a patient suffering from cataracts.

Natural church development uses the church profile to:

The Benefits of a Church Profile

• help your church discover its critical factor for the development of the church and its current situation.

• focus limited resources (human, financial, etc.) at the critical points.

• identify your church's strengths and the weaknesses.

• save time and eliminate the risk of an inaccurate analysis.

• apply a scientific and exact process developed by social scientists.

• provide you with an outside perspective—how does your church compare with other churches?

Finding the Subjects Whose Timing Is Right

We are often contacted by churches that want seminars on a specific subject, "gifts," or "inspiring church services," or any other aspect of natural church development that might promise some progress. We respond by saying that while such a seminar might be informative and interesting for some of the church members, it might not help them much in their future development. Since we do not want to do what we recommend others to avoid, there are no seminars where there has not been a church analysis. Is that stubbornness? You could try my old glasses.

Your Thoughts

• *In this chapter you have learned about some of the benefits of developing a church profile. If you are still skeptical about it, it might help to reverse the perspective and ask: What advantages would there be to not develop an accurate church profile in our situation? Write down any advantages that come to your mind!*

How To Proceed

Now we come to the practical part: How do you actually conduct a survey in order to develop a church profile?

First you will need only the questionnaires: There are thirty sheets for those who work within your church, and one for the pastor. To do the church profile, follow the following steps carefully:

Step 1: Yellow Questionnaire

The yellow questionnaire should be filled out by the senior pastor. If your church does not have a full-time pastor, or no person with the title of "pastor", this survey should be completed by that person on your leadership team who seems to be the one in charge of making sure that everything in the church comes together.

Step 2: Green Questionnaire

The green questionnaires are to be filled out by volunteer workers of your church. Whenever possible, at least thirty people should complete them. While the number of questionnaires can be reduced a bit for smaller churches, note that the results of the survey will be markedly less reliable.

"Everybody who fills out a questionnaire should know exactly what the purpose of this activity is."

All your workers who fill out a questionnaire should have, if possible, the following characteristics:

a. The pastor considers them to be actively involved at *the very center of church life.*

b. They should have a *regular task* in the church.

c. They should be a member of a small group in the church (a cell group, Bible study group, ministry team, etc.)

It works best to allow thirty minutes to complete the questionnaires during a routinely scheduled meeting that already includes the persons described above. All completed questionnaires are immediately collected and turned over to the designated person. This survey should not be conducted without giving your coworkers some basic information. In the context of such a meeting, they can then be informed about the reason, purpose, and process of this action. Questions can be discussed immediately. The questionnaires could be distributed in the context of an information seminar conducted in your church.

In any case, every person that fills out the questionnaire should know the church has decided to take this step. The booklet *The ABC's of Natural Church Development* can help you in this task. Many churches have had a good experience by handing out this booklet to everyone filling out the questionnaire. The booklet summarizes the most important principles of natural church development in just a few pages, and underlines the importance of a church profile. It can be read in about twenty minutes.

When you have received all the completed questionnaires, you have several possibilities of how to get your results:

Step 3: Evaluation

a. You can return the questionnaires to the organization, consultant, or trainer from whom you received it. You will find their address on the information sheet that came with the questionnaires. In two to four weeks you will receive your church profile with suggestions, including how to improve your minimum factor. The interpretation will refer to the text of this book and include suggestions for the next steps in your situation.

b. You can purchase the full software version of CORE if you attend a Natural Church Development Basic Training event. After inputting the responses, your church profile can be processed at the touch of a button and printed out immediately. This option is best for churches that work frequently with the church profile and therefore value immediate results. If you have the software, it would be possible to organize an introductory meeting about natural church development, hand out the questionnaires, have the participants fill them out, then process and print out a church profile during the same meeting. We also recommend the purchase of the software package, CORE, for church consultants, organizations or denominations that wish to support local churches in the practical steps of church development.

> *CORE is the software program that calculates your church profile. The program is based on a formula that builds on the results of all churches researched so far.*
>
> See NCD, pages 109, 122-23

Current prices and addresses come with the information included with the questionnaires.

Next you should *implement* those steps described above that fit your situation the best. We recommend that you do another church profile in six to twelve months so you can see how your current minimum factor has developed over time. You will also be able to identify the new minimum factor of your church.

Step 4: Implementation

Your Thoughts:

• *When will we do a church profile?*

• *Whom do we have to convince before we can implement this plan in our church?*

• *What possible resistance could people have against doing a church profile?*

• *How will I deal with this resistance?*

• *How will I inform the church members about the survey and its usefulness for our church?*

❏ Seminar/Information meeting

❏ The booklet *The ABC's of Natural Church Development*

❏ Other needs:

Interpreting Your Church Profile

After you have calculated your church profile scores, you will know the current condition of the growth potential of your church, and exactly where to start strengthening your church so it can experience new qualitative and quantitative growth. The church profile informs you about the strength of eight quality characteristics (see Part 3). Our research indicates that these characteristics clearly distinguish growing churches from declining churches (we use abbreviations as used by CORE software):

- Empowering leadership (LE)

- Gift-oriented ministry (MI)

- Passionate spirituality (SP)

- Functional structures (ST)

- Inspiring worship service (WO)

- Holistic small groups (SM)

- Need-oriented evangelism (EV)

- Loving relationships (RE)

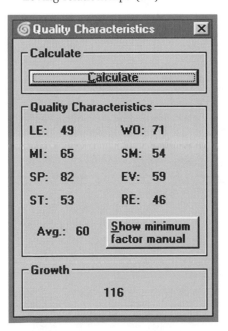

When you give CORE the command to calculate the profile scores (instructions for the use of CORE come with the software package) you will receive the results first as numbers (see illustration). "Avg." indicates the average value of your eight scores. "Growth" is a growth index based on your reported church attendance figures. It serves only for research purposes when a church growth consultant analyzes your growth. If you have access to a spreadsheet with graphic capabilities the profile scores can also be reproduced as informative bar graphs (see illustration on page 16). Then you can decide how to represent your church profile scores most effectively in a graphic and informative way.

What the Scores Mean Each profile score has been calculated on the basis of a number of questions contained in the questionnaire. These scores represent—as a statistician would say—standard scores, which are based on a mean of 50 with a standard deviation of 15. What does this mean for your church? Simply this: the average score of a quality characteristic for an average church is 50. But a deviation of plus or minus 15 is common.

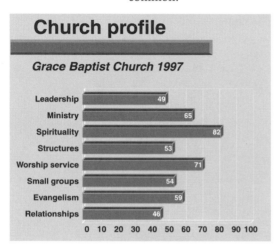

Church profile

Grace Baptist Church 1997

Leadership	49
Ministry	65
Spirituality	82
Structures	53
Worship service	71
Small groups	54
Evangelism	59
Relationships	46

0 10 20 30 40 50 60 70 80 90 100

Therefore, if the scores of your church profile move between 35 and 65, they are like those of most churches—sometimes a little better, sometimes a little weaker. The fact that your church has a minimum factor does not suggest that you are a bad church. Even the best churches have a minimum factor. The minimum factor only indicates an area that should receive special attention in your future efforts to strengthen the growth potential of your church.

A score above 65 indicates above-average quality. A score below 35 indicates problems that cannot be ignored (or at least a data problem). The eight scores are a dependable basis for responsible church growth planning. Sometimes, however, it might be interesting to analyze data more in depth (e.g. mid scores, response frequency, specific questions, etc.) CORE is based on complex scientific foundations that do not allow this kind of analysis to be done by yourself. A detailed analysis can be done for you through ChurchSmart Resources. Contact ChurchSmart Resources for more information and current pricing.

The Adjectives Are Crucial In all eight areas measured by the church profile, the key ingredient is always the qualifying adjective. Take a look at the church profile picture on this page. You might notice first that "spirituality" and "worship service" reflect above-average quality, while the scores for "relationships" and "leadership" are fairly normal. However, this church profile measures neither "spirituality," nor "relationships," nor "worship service," nor "leadership." What is measured is the *degree* to which a church works "biotically" in any of these areas.

> *"Working biotically":*
> *an abbreviation for the*
> *continuous application of the*
> *six biotic principles in each*
> *area of your church.*
>
> See NCD, pages 61-82

In this church, "worship" is intensely "passionate." This adjective refers to the way a church is involved in putting all six biotic principles into practice, which leads its members to perceive their worship as "inspiring." Every church is led, has people involved in ministry, and conducts a worship service. When these areas are examined, the decisive question is: *How well is* the church doing in this area? The leadership in our example is not very "empowering" and the relationships are "loving" at just an average level.

From the perspective of natural church development, the quality criteria always reflect to what degree biotic principles, summarized by each of the adjectives, are at work in this area.

Your Thoughts:

• *The following quality characteristic is currently the minimum factor of your church:*

• *The minimum factor score of _____ is*

❏ *within average range (between 35 and 65)*

❏ *above average positive (over 65)*

❏ *below average negative (below 35)*

• *How do you feel about these results? Do they describe your church accurately?*

• *Would it be helpful to contact a church consultant or request a detailed analysis?*

Monitoring Your Progress

"There is little gained in doing a church profile only once."

Some churches are reluctant to check their progress in church development. After some conflicts, the decision is finally made to do a church profile. The results are received and lead to the decision to improve the minimum factor. But the last step, checking progress, can be shortcircuited by the remark: "Our last profile is only a few months old, why do another one now?" Wherever this step is skipped, the church robs itself of the important experience of monitoring its progress in church development.

Consequences of Failing to Check Progress

Some time ago, our institute worked with a local church which had been quite enthusiastic about natural church development, and had done a church profile nine months earlier. They assured us that they had worked intensively to improve their minimum factor. However, the church was still losing members. A new church profile revealed that the minimum factor was still the same, but the scores were lower than before. During a feedback session the source of this surprising result was revealed: they had discussed numerous steps they wanted to take *without ever implementing them.* Their discussions had created the impression that something was being done, but in reality, nothing had changed.

*Monitoring the progress of natural church development means finding out, **to what extent have the applied measures been fruitful?** One way this can be done is by doing another church profile.*

See NCD, pages 120-121

Another church had worked hard to improve its minimum factor, "gift-oriented ministry." They could see visible fruit from their efforts. The most obvious sign of their success was that they had overcome a shortage of team workers in almost all areas of ministry, and the workers were much more motivated than before. Since their success was so evident, church leaders felt that no new church profile was needed. But then something curious happened. The church started to lose members again. The pastor and his leaders were at a loss to explain this. They decided to have another church profile done which revealed the problem: While the quality factor "gift-oriented ministry" had indeed improved markedly, the quality of "functional structures" had sagged and become their new minimum factor.

Discover Mistakes During the Implementation

Further analysis showed that while the church had been working in the area "gift-oriented ministry," it had made a significant mistake. Church leaders had indeed helped members discover their gifts. They had offered gift counseling and help in finding tasks where members could use their gifts. But they had neither developed a support structure for their workers nor pulled them together into teams. That meant that they had many people in the church with a job that matched their giftedness, but they were isolated in their ministry.

Like lone rangers, they had neither team support nor coaches to turn to for help when problems arose. Many lacked even the basic information needed to execute their task well. All these factors contributed to a fading of their initial enthusiasm and a gradual drop in membership. Fortunately, this church has learned from its experiences and checks its situation regularly through a church profile.

Progress can be monitored with the current version of CORE simply by comparing two or more church profiles (instructions about how to use the software are included with the package of the program diskette). After loading the files for your last two church profiles, you can convert the resulting change scores into a plus-minus graph in your spreadsheet.

How CORE Helps You Monitor Progress

In this type of graph (see box), you can see quickly which area has improved in quality and how successful your steps toward church development have actually been. But you can also spot those areas that still need more qualitative development.

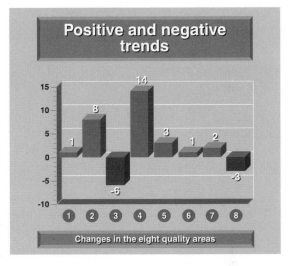

Changes in the eight quality areas

Churches are constantly changing. New people join. Others leave. Christians themselves change. Contextual factors impact a local church. Society leaves its marks. Spiritual movements come and go. Workers and leaders imprint a church for a time. Church growth programs are implemented or ignored. A church is never just frozen in a *status quo*.

Over a Period of Several Years

If you want to stay on the cutting edge of church development, it is important to observe changes over longer time periods. There is not much sense in doing a church profile just once, either as a tool for crisis management or because of pure curiosity. But even if a second church profile has been conducted to evaluate progress, the true usefulness of this analysis tool is not exhausted. Church *development* takes place where long-term processes are pursued, implemented and continually monitored.

Your Thoughts:

• *When will you check the success of your work to improve the minimum factor?*

Why Intuition Is Often Misleading

Some people think they know what's wrong with a church: "In our church there is a lack of love!" or "If we would pray more and have stronger faith . . ." Most Christians feel that they know their church quite well and consequently assume they also know what needs to be done to develop their church. Thus, what new insights could possibly be gained from doing a church profile?

"Networking the perspectives of many individuals results in an accurate picture."

The problem is that each member—and even the pastor—see only part of the total picture or reality. What they point out may be accurate, but may still be only part of the total picture. Only when they link their different partial views together into a holistic perspective do they gain an accurate picture.

This is where the church profile comes in. The different perceptions of thirty workers and the pastor combine through a complex formula into a new whole. This world formula is an extract of all those churches that have been surveyed so far: more than five thousand churches in more than thirty countries. In this formula, we have inserted middle scores and standard deviations for different countries, as well as the individual answers of church members for whom the church profile was done.

In this way, the church profile offers exact results. "Exact" does not mean that the church has been evaluated "objectively," that is, independent from the perspective of those who are part of the church's team. In fact, it is this subjective perspective that determines the attitudes of those who work in the church and their approach to problems. The church survey serves to objectify the subjective perspectives.

CORE uses a built-in "world formula" to calculate an individual church profile for each church. This formula is based on the survey results of more than five thousand churches which are compared to the data of each local church that is being analyzed.

See NCD, pages 108-109

Some time ago, we received a call from the pastor of a church that had conducted a church survey. When the church profile scores arrived from our institute, one of the church members also added up all the answers "manually," and was amazed that the results were completely different. This did not surprise us for several reasons: first, during the "self-scoring" procedure many questions were assigned to the wrong quality characteristics. Second, they used an arbitrary scoring key. Third, this procedure also ignored the impact of negative formulations in questions (or positive questions were wrongly counted as negative ones). Fourth, they didn't have the "world formula" necessary to correctly convert raw scores into profile scores. And even if they had all the information necessary, the process of calculating all these scores would have taken days to complete. This is why our institute uses the special software program that has been developed specifically to produce church profiles.

A similar experience was reported to us by a church consultant from Australia. His E-mail message started with: "I am quite confused about the results of the church profile . . . " The profile did not at all fit the church he was working with. When we reviewed the procedures he had followed to do the church profile, we found that he had not used CORE, which is based on the worldwide church growth survey, but a spreadsheet worksheet he had designed himself to do the calculations.

Even Inaccurate Tests May Be Popular

In extreme cases, wrong score results are not even noticed. A few years ago a team of psychologists asked a group of managers to fill out a personality test. Afterwards, without the knowledge of the managers, they mixed the results in such a way that none of the people tested received his or her own profile. Still, more than 90 percent of the respondents said that they could identify with the test results! Even in the context of church surveys, there are tests that have the quality of horoscopes, and yet they are accepted.

Church development is possible without computer programs, handbooks, and church consultants. However, if you plan to find out which of the eight quality characteristics is your current minimum factor, you should carefully select a method that has been developed on the basis of a sufficiently large database. Only in this way will you ensure that you have a scoring key that has been adjusted properly. If you skip this step, you are in danger of receiving results that will not be very reliable. In many cases, it would have been better to rely on a completely subjective self analysis: "What do you think is our minimum factor?"

Your Thoughts:

- *A subjective self-evaluation of the church members can be valuable to sharpen problem consciousness, but it should not be confused with conducting a survey for a church profile. What would you designate right now as your church's minimum factor? Does this view agree with the results of the church profile?*

Ten Action Steps

Natural church development is not a single action with a static beginning and ending point. Rather, it is a process that shapes the life of the church over the long term. How can this process be nurtured? This section is designed to offer practical help in implementing in your own church the 10-step program described in the book Natural Church Development on pages 103-125.

The Step Before the First Step

"Your own goals will determine, to a large extent, which practical steps you will take."

Before you begin applying the following practical steps, you should have a clear notion of the purpose of this venture. Terms such as "church development" or "church growth" can be—and are!—defined differently by various groups of Christians. So what is the goal that motivated you to deal with this subject more intensively?

1. Is your goal to get more people to attend the church service—by any means necessary?

2. Are you trying to realize—within existing structures which you regard as hindering but unchangeable—at least partial aspects of the church of Jesus Christ?

3. Is your goal to reform, as consistently as possible, those structures which hinder the growth of your congregation?

4. Are you trying to raise confidence in the process of church development in a church which tends to view this subject rather suspiciously?

5. If your church has grown significantly over the last few years, do you want to pay increased attention to quality factors in the church?

6. Do you wish that your stagnating or shrinking church would experience growth again?

7. Is your goal for your seemingly healthy church to preserve this health also in the future?

8. Are you hoping that your church will birth other churches?

9. Do you hope to begin planting a new church without the help of a mother church?

Which Goal Is "Right"?

Over and over again we are asked which of these goals are right—in view of natural church development—and which are not. Any of the goals mentioned above can be "right" for you. And you can use the principles of natural church development to accomplish any of these goals. But they must be *your* own—not the model goals you find in a textbook. Your individual goals will determine, to a large degree, which steps you will take to implement the approach of natural church development in your own church. For this reason, you should clarify this question before you proceed with any steps.

Imagine the following situation. Your church is characterized by a theology which is totally incompatible with missionary outreach, as well as by an ossified church structure. What does this particular institutional context mean for your church development plans? Do you attack the prevailing theology and the structure of your church?

Or do you define your concern rather cautiously, without questioning existing structures, in order to create a more favorable climate for church development in your own context?

Both ways are possible. How you approach a situation will depend to a large extent on your own goals. If you have adopted goal 3 in the list of goals above, you will invariably expose exactly those factors which are the causes for the troubles of your churches. But if you proceed from goal 4, your answer might be exactly the opposite. You will avoid subjects that tend to irritate people, you will proceed most cautiously, and you will try to link any new ideas with existing traditions and doctrines. Your goal is not to radically change church structures, but to do as much as possible—within the existing framework—for the fulfillment of the Great Commission.

Different Goals— Different Approaches

The following ten steps can be applied for the most different goals. How you will use these ideas, however, will depend strongly on your vision of what you want to accomplish.

 ## Your Thoughts:

• *With which of these goals can you identify most?*

❏ 1. Increasing worship attendance

❏ 2. Developing your church within existing parameters

❏ 3. Overcoming barriers to church growth

❏ 4. Developing trust in church development

❏ 5. Emphasizing quality factors in rapidly growing churches

❏ 6. Leading non-growing churches towards growth

❏ 7. Developing the health of the church further

❏ 8. Planting daughter churches

❏ 9. Starting a new church

You may have completely different goals for church development. Then you should write these goals down.

Build Spiritual Momentum

"Teach people the longing for the wide, boundless ocean."

Antoine de Saint-Exupéry has said: "If you want to build a ship, don't summon people to buy wood, prepare tools, distribute jobs, and organize the work, rather teach people the yearning for the wide, boundless ocean."

You could not find a better way to define this first step. While steps 2 through 10 concern those things similar to Saint-Exupéry's "summon people, buy wood, prepare tools, distribute jobs, and organize the work," the first step starts at a more fundamental level: the yearning to realize God's purpose for your own church. Steps 2 through 10 begin where this yearning has already taken root, but they are not necessarily the best steps to actually awaken this yearning. To do a church profile, for instance, may be a good way to help those who are already captivated by this yearning to turn into reality what has already started to grow in their heart. But it is hardly useful to create this yearning.

An Enduring Concern for Every Church

The question of motivation for church development can't be overlooked. It is not a subject to be checked off once, in order to move to the next subject. In some churches, Christians have never developed this yearning; in other churches this yearning started years ago but has decreased over time. In still other churches, there are groups of Christians with a deep spiritual yearning who ask: "What can we do to spread this to even more Christians?"

Helps From Outside the Church Growth Movement

Fortunately, there are many resources available to further spiritual motivation and set it free. A lot of these resources have not been created within the church growth paradigm, and have little to do with it. Quite often, we even find some critical remarks that devalue the technical aspects of church development. In many instances, these resources speak the language of the "spiritualizing paradigm." Still, if these resources help to rekindle a new spiritual passion, they have fulfilled their purpose.

On the following page, you will find a list of suggestions that will enable you to help as many members as possible find a new spiritual motivation in their lives. Not all suggestions may be applicable for you. You will probably find quite a few that are not even on the list.

"Spiritual momentum" does not refer here to the quality characteristic "passionate spirituality," but to the motivation why we are concerned about the subject of church development in the first place. See NCD, pages 106-107

Your Thoughts:

• *Go through the following list and ask yourself, "Which of these steps or suggestions might be useful to instill a new spiritual yearning for God in our congregation?" Use this sheet to write down any concrete applications that come to your mind.*

❏ Study the life of a model church.

Which one?

❏ Visit an inspiring church service outside your own congregation.

Where?

❏ Invite a motivating guest speaker.

Whom?

❏ Go on a spiritual retreat to ask questions of personal faith.

With whom?

❏ Prepare a sermon series focused on developing a yearning for God.

When?

❏ Visit a large, inspiring Christian event.

Which one?

❏ Encounter a Christian community.

Which one?

❏ Study devotional literature with someone.

What material?

❏ Use pastoral resources in your home church.

Which?

Other:

Step 2: Determine Your Minimum Factors

"The picture of the minimum barrel is a simple demonstration of the minimum strategy."

The reasons for the strategic importance of identifying the minimum factors in your church have been discussed at length in the book *Natural Church Development*, and will not be repeated here. With the help of the picture of the minimum barrel, we can demonstrate their significance even to people who are not necessarily interested in questions of church development.

The first part of this workbook describes different possible approaches in this step, several options for scoring the results, as well as how to interpret the results. In Part 5, and also in Appendix 2, you will find background information about the scientific basis for this survey. When you get ready to actually do a church profile, you should have all these resources ready to answer questions or deal with misunderstandings.

Minimum Factors are those quality characteristics of a church which are developed the least and block the growth of the church.

See NCD, pages 49-60, 108-109

 Your Thoughts:

• *Indicate here which factor the church profile identified as the minimum factor of your church. If there are several quality characteristics that score similarly low, it could be useful to fill in two (but not more!) factors where you will want to concentrate your energies in the future.*

• *When has this church profile been done?*

• *Which factor(s) surfaced as the minimum factor(s)?*

Step 3: Set Qualitative Goals

"For each step, define the concrete results expected."

With the church profile, you also receive pointers for practical steps you can take to improve the minimum factor. These suggestions are relatively general—a consequence of the principle-oriented approach of natural church development. In this way, we avoid forcing church-es to labor through prepackaged sets of methods which do not fit their situation.

By taking a good look at your church and at the checklists of possi-ble steps you will have to think through—possibly with the help of a church consultant—you can better determine which of these sugges-tions should be taken up and in what ways they should be applied or modified. For each adopted measure, you should formulate concrete goals of what you expect to see as a result. They should be specific, not general. "Conduct the evangelism seminar," is too general. This one, "To have 10 percent of the participants of the evangelism semi-nar discover the gift of evangelism by the end of the year, and to have a personal session with each participant about how he or she can use his gifts more effectively towards fulfilling the Great Commission," is specific.

On page 111 of the book *Natural Church Development,* you will find examples for each of the quality characteristics and proper qualitative goals. In each case, the key is to make concrete progress in one or more of the quality areas of the church.

Your Thoughts:

• *On the worksheet on the next page, list about five qualitative goals for your minimum factor. You may find some inspiration from the list of suggestions for your minimum factor which you will find in the third part of the book. Don't be afraid to be playful. Word the goals in such a way that they fit your particular situation.*

Take into account that goals should have the fol-lowing criteria: a) Address a concrete area of needed progress in the development of the church, b) have a time criterion, c) be results that can be measured.

Please do not yet think about all the possible barriers that might hinder the fulfilling of these goals. Dwelling on hindering circum-stances too early is one of the strongest hindering blocks to finding new, creative solutions.

*In the context of natural church development **qualita-tive goals** represent those precise, time oriented, and controllable goals which aim at increasing the quality of the church.*

See NCD, pages 110-111

Worksheet: Qualitative Goals

We can expect a significant quality improvement in our minimum factor by reaching the following goals:

Goal 1: _____

_____

Date: _____

Result: _____

Goal 2: _____

_____

Date: _____

Result: _____

Goal 3: _____

_____

Date: _____

Result: _____

Goal 4: _____

_____

Date: _____

Result: _____

Goal 5: _____

_____

Date: _____

Result: _____

Step 4: Identify Obstacles

When you begin to put qualitative goals into practice, you will encounter problems. These problems can consist of external factors (such as a lack of space). In most cases, however, resistance will come from other Christians.

Some resistance is simply due to ignorance. It is amazing how much skepticism dissolves when you take the time to explain the principles of natural church development in a comprehensive way to other people.

Unfortunately, few of your difficulties will belong to this category. Part of the resistance is based on psychological-relational difficulties, while another part is due to "paradigm blocks." Much of the opposition to natural church development—often couched in theological language—is ultimately due to a mindset of some Christians which we have called the "spiritualizing" and the "technocratic" paradigms, respectively. This is the reason why we addressed this problem so much in the book *Natural Church Development*.

Resistance, which results from a lack of information, should not be dealt with as a pastoral problem. Trying to solve psycho-relational problems with more information is futile. That's why it is critical that you analyze carefully the category of problem you are trying to solve.

Finally, let us give you a bitter pill of truth: Paradigm blocks can't be solved by more information nor by pastoral counseling. Although every Christian who has discovered traces of a questionable mindset in his own thinking can work for a paradigm shift in his or her own life, this can't be done for somebody else.

"Paradigm blocks cannot be solved through gaining information nor pastoral counseling."

How to Deal With Paradigm Blocks

Wherever you feel that certain blocks are caused primarily by paradigm reasons, don't even try to lead people through a paradigm shift. The methods often suggested in management books—"How to effect a paradigm change in other people"—are either unrealistic (they promise what simply does not work) or they tend to step over the important border towards manipulation (the next step after that is called "brainwashing"). People have an allergic reaction to any attempt to being manipulated. This reaction is usually a sign of a healthy mind.

The spiritualizing paradigm is a mental model that spiritually devalues the significance of organizational matters, rational thinking, and empirical study.

See NCD, pages 90-91, 94-95, 98-99, 112-113

In short: Pastoral problems deserve pastoral attention, information deficits should be addressed with information. But how do you deal with paradigm blocks in other Christians? Leave the miracle of changing someone's paradigm to God. Yes, such miracles happen from time to time. But in our experience, the probability that they happen

> *The **technocratic paradigm** is the illusion that by employing certain methods, the church of Jesus Christ can be produced. Technocratic thinking shows up as a traditionalist variant, or as a church growth variant ("Just use this method!")*
>
> See NCD, pages 88-89, 94-95, 98-99, 112-113

decreases proportionally with our efforts to force them on someone.

By contrast: the more effort we invest into the quality of relationships, the better the pastoral care processes in our church, the higher the level of knowledge about natural church development, the sooner our church will be the nurturing soil on which such unexpected paradigm shifts do happen!

Your Thoughts:

• *First take one of the qualitative goals you wrote down on page 30 and copy it into the first line on the following page. Then list possible hindrances which (could) stand in the way of reaching the goal. Try to assign the problems to one of the following categories: a) Lack of information, b) psycho-relational problem, c) paradigm block, and d) something else.*

Example: An expected power struggle would belong to category b; the reference to the high costs of a suggested step would possibly be a category a problem; the argument "But this is not spiritual" indicates category c; the sickness of a staff member falls under category d. In many cases you will find that the different categories actually are linked to one and the same problem. In this case, it is especially helpful to notice the different roots that feed the arguments of the opposition.

Next, use this same process to deal with all the other goals in your list on page 30. You will find a worksheet that you can copy on the following page.

Worksheet: How to Deal with Resistance

Describe the goal that should be reached:

_____

_____

Barrier 1: _____

Kind of barrier:

❏ Lack of information   ❏ Paradigm block

❏ Psycho-relational problem   ❏ Something else:

Possible steps to overcome the resistance:

_____

_____

Barrier 2: _____

Kind of barrier:

❏ Lack of information   ❏ Paradigm block

❏ Psycho-relational problem   ❏ Something else:

Possible steps to overcome the resistance:

_____

_____

Barrier 3: _____

Kind of barrier:

❏ Lack of information   ❏ Paradigm block

❏ Psycho-relational problem   ❏ Something else:

Possible steps to overcome the resistance:

_____

_____

**Part 2:
Implementation**

Step 5: Apply biotic principles

"The biotic principles give us something like a "sixth sense"—a sense of God's growth automatisms."

Natural church development has nothing to do with effecting church growth through mere human effort. Rather we should direct our steps toward releasing God's growth automatisms more fully than before. In the book *Natural Church Development*, we show extensively why we as human beings can work quite well towards improving the quality of our church, while the quantitative growth (in church attendance, membership, conversions) belongs to the area that resists human striving.

Here, the negative influence of two wrong but widespread theological paradigms becomes obvious. While the "spiritualizers" declare even the quality of a church as a sphere that evades human creative influence, the "technocrats" tend to view quantitative growth as the result of human activity. The mindset of representatives from either camp does not allow them to understand the importance of the term "growth automatism"—a key term in natural church development. In our experience, the spiritual and strategic significance of this concept unfolds only where people start to think in terms of the new, bipolar, biotic paradigm.

Biotic principles are principles that are have been borrowed from the living world (Greek bios = life) and whose conscious or unconscious application can be found in growing churches.

See NCD, pages 61-82, 114-115

God's growth automatisms (a rather abstract sounding term at first) can be studied—in creation as well as in the church—by looking at those biotic principles which apply the term "growth automatism" to the everyday life in the church. In Part 4 of this handbook you will find a training program that will increase your abilities to make decisions in harmony with biotic principles. This training has been designed to be used by individuals or groups of Christians—the church leaders for instance. Whoever goes through this training will be able to make decisions according to natural church development principles. As time goes by you will develop a kind of "sixth sense," a special sensitivity for God's growth automatisms.

 Your Thoughts:

• *When do you plan to conduct the program described above? With whom?*

Step 6: Exercise Your Strengths

Focusing the strengths of a church to work on the minimum factor is an immensely powerful principle. Of course, not everything that you could identify in your church as a "strength" can be used directly to improve the quality of your minimum factor. But it pays to carefully survey all areas of church life to identify (potentially hidden) strengths that could be used for this purpose.

To the degree that you succeed in directing the energy of your God-given strengths towards the least developed quality areas in your church, you will experience how much the church seems to develop "all by itself."

"When you apply this principle you will experience how much the church seems to develop "all by itself".

 Your Thoughts:

• *In the following list, note each point that you consider a strength of the church.*

❏ The maximum factors of your church (according to the church profile).

❏ Aspects of the spiritual culture in your church that could positively influence the work on the minimum factor.

❏ Contextual factors (that is factors in the environment of the church) which could be used for work on the minimum factor.

❏ Spiritual gifts among Christians which are needed especially for the work on your minimum factor.

❏ Other strengths which could be relevant for the work on the minimum factor.

• *Write down what would need to be done in order to put these strengths to work on the minimum factor.*

The term maximum factors designates those quality characteristics in a church that are developed the strongest.
See NCD, pages 56-57, 116-117

Step 7: Use Biotic Tools

"The subject of church growth is approached consciously from the perspective of the everyday life of a Christian."

There is a world of difference between the strategic work of church leaders and the everyday life of church members. To address the second category, our institute is in the process of developing tools for each of the eight quality characteristics. Their aim is to strengthen the quality in each area by consistently using the principles of natural church development.

Natural Church Development and the *Natural Church Development Implementation Guide* have been written in a rather compressed and non-narrative style using numerous technical terms and operating on the basis of scientific research findings. But these eight practical books are quite different. While the principles of natural church development are their basis, we do not discuss them systematically. Nor do we use most of the technical terms of natural church development ("biotic principles," "minimum factor," etc.) if we can avoid it. Instead of presenting our arguments on the basis of research findings, we proceed mostly in narrative form, using stories, anecdotes, and actual experiences. In these books, the needs of the individual Christian are our central concern. We consciously do not approach the topic of church growth from the perspective of church leaders ("How can we improve the quality of this minimum factor?") but from the every day perspective of Christians in the marketplace ("How can I experience growth in this area?").

Biotic tools are resources that spell out the natural church development approach for the daily work in the church.
See NCD, pages 118-119

The resources in this series are designed to be especially useful for small groups. The results we have observed so far in churches that have adopted these processes speak for themselves: In most cases that succeeded in involving over 50 percent of those attending worship into biotic growth processes, we observed that the current minimum factor was transformed into the new maximum factor.

 Your Thoughts:

• *The following resources for natural church development could assist us in our work on the minimum factor:*

• *Which of our small groups should we win to work with these resource tools?*

Step 8: Monitor Effectiveness

In order to integrate natural church development into the long-term life of the church, it is important to make regular feedback part of the lifestyle of those leading the ministry of the church. No worship service, no church program or activity should pass without the responsible leaders asking themselves afterwards: "What could we improve next time?" The big problem is that feedback—positive or negative—is often neglected in many churches. Lack of feedback frustrates co-workers, prevents critical but fruitful interaction within the ministry team, and finally institutionalizes mediocrity in the church.

"Lack of feedback frustrates co-workers and institutionalizes mediocrity in the church."

The first part of this workbook (on pages 10-22) details how taking a church profile in regular intervals can monitor qualitative growth. The switch from action-oriented to process-oriented church development will succeed only if a good system of monitoring progress gets anchored in the everyday operation of the church.

One of the easiest means to monitor effectiveness in church development is to conduct a new church profile survey and compare the results with the previous one.

See NCD, pages 120-121

Your Thoughts:

• *Here are some examples of good progress-monitoring feedback. Check those ideas which you think would (should) also work in your church. For each point you do not check, please indicate the advantages for not using this particular system.*

❏ Doing a new church profile

❏ Observing and analyzing church attendance

❏ Regular reference to the quality factor checklists in Part 3 of this book

❏ Feedback meetings after each church activity

❏ Feedback meetings with every team member

❏ Other:

Step 9: Address Your New Minimum Factors

"One of the eight quality characteristics is always the current minimum factor."

Sometimes we are asked how long a church should focus on natural church development. This question reflects clearly how much our thinking is fixed on church activities, programs, and models.

Will there ever be a time when the church will no longer work on empowering people for service, commissioning the gifts of Christians for ministry, encouraging joyful faith, reforming church structures, improving worship services, multiplying small groups, intensifying evangelistic efforts, or intensifying Christian love bonds? All these things belong to the basic commission of any church—until Jesus comes again.

Natural church development is not action oriented, but process oriented. All its measures aim at long-term organic development processes that organize themselves.

See NCD, pages 122-123

There are always certain areas that merit special attention of the church leadership. One of the eight quality characteristics is always the current minimum factor of your church. And improving the quality of your minimum factor is always the goal. For this reason we can never aim at being finished with natural church development. What can happen is that you enter a phase where a multitude of difficulties and barriers that surfaced during the beginning phase no longer exist. Moreover, the church may, thankfully, find that what in the beginning seemed to require enormous energy investments now seems to happen "all by itself."

This is the key: The more we make sure that all the steps we are taking are characterized by the principle of "self-organization," the more likely it is that in the long term you will see self-supporting growth structures that outlive even the change of charismatic leaders.

 Your Thoughts:

• *What is the new minimum factor of your church?*

• *What measures are necessary to improve the quality in the area concerned?*

Step 10: Multiply Your Church

Not every church will multiply by birthing new churches, but every church that does not should have good reasons for this decision. Just as it is a rule in God's creation that healthy creatures reproduce and thus multiply, it should also be a normal rule for churches.

In the book *Natural Church Development*, we have shown that for most churches, it is neither possible nor a desirable goal to grow to the size of a megachurch. The "big church" should normally not be our model. In view of our findings, the challenge of continuous church multiplication has acquired new urgency.

Churches with 1000 or more in attendance are the exceptions. By contrast, the rule should be churches of about 100 to 200 attendees who continuously help new churches to be born. This is demonstrably the most effective contribution a church can make to world evangelization.

"The rule should be churches with 100 to 200 in attendance which are birthing other churches."

Your Thoughts:

• *The following is a list of different situations that apply to churches that have begun to implement natural church development principles. If any of these conditions ever applies to you, perhaps church planting might be your next new step.*

❏ Your church owes its origin to a relatively recent church planting project that has evidently prospered.

❏ Even though your church has above aver age quality scores on all quality characteristics (all over 50) it has reached a natural growth barrier. Quantitative growth is stagnating.

❏ You have made a conscious decision that you will stay a small church, but you want to continue to be involved in reaching people with the love of God.

❏ All eight scores of the church profile measure 65 or above. Such a profile usually indicates great church planting potential.

In the context of natural church development, church planting is not to be understood as aggressiveness against existing churches, but rather as a normal and desirable consequence of organic development processes.

See NCD, pages 124-125

How to Improve Your Minimum Factor

The church profile has helped you discover which of the quality characteristics of growing churches is presently your minimum factor. But what can you do to increase the quality in this area? In this part you will find suggestions for each of the eight quality characteristics.

The Personality of Your Church

"Not every suggestion will be just the right step for your situation at this time."

The ideas in the following chapters assume that you have already developed a church profile and want to focus your main attention on your minimum factor. We have consciously avoided step-by-step programs for each of the quality characteristics, because it would never do justice to the individuality of each different church situation. You must therefore "individualize" each idea yourself and relate it to the concrete situation of your church. You will also have to choose among several ideas. Not every suggestion will be the right step for your situation at this point in time. Which of the ideas you will select and in which order you develop them will depend on different factors, for instance:

The Score of Your Minimum Factor

• *How strong or how weak is your minimum factor?* If the score is less than 35, most of the suggested measures will be virgin territory for you. You should carefully consider which of the necessary steps will be received with the greatest openness. And you will have to invest a lot of time for the work in this area. Is your score more than 65? Then even in the area of your minimum factor, you are already a model for other churches! It is, however, still an area which deserves your special attention. You may have already put into practice many of the suggested measures. As you work with this factor, your goal is not to introduce completely new things, but to take a critical look at what is already done, and renew and reform. Use the checklists in each chapter to ask yourself: "What could we improve in this area in the future?"

The Character of the Church

• *What is the character of your church and its style to express spirituality?* Your attempts to improve the "passionate spirituality" factor will be very different if your church home is a non-charismatic Baptist church, or if you lead a Pentecostal church. The possibilities for making progress in improving the "functional structures" factor will be different if you work in a traditional Lutheran church which has existed for decades, or if the church profile is part of a church planting project. It is important to understand that the principles are the same in all circumstances—how you apply these principles may differ markedly.

Previous Experience with Natural Church Development

• *What is the level of your previous experience with natural church development?* Have you already worked for years, consciously applying these principles, or is this whole approach something rather new for you? If you have already worked with these principles you will be able to immediately put new ideas into practice. You already worked at improving a minimum factor with obvious success. This positive experience is a good link to your current reality. If you are considering this approach seriously for the first time, you may have to invest considerable time to communicate basic information about natural church development. "What is a minimum factor anyway?" "Why do a church profile?" "What is so significant about those eight quality characteristics?" Or maybe even more basic: "Why strive to build up and develop your church?" "Is it not enough if the Word is preached and people receive pastoral care?" You can anticipate many other questions.

In the framework of natural church development only those factors that have a proven, positive correlation with quantitative growth and whose practical application furthers church growth are defined as universal principles. See NCD, pages 16-19, 58-60

- *Why has the new church profile resulted in the same minimum factor as the previous church profile?* It is possible—after you have identified a certain minimum factor through a first church profile and spent time to improve it, and after you did a second church profile—to discover: It is still that same minimum factor. This should indicate to you the importance of continuing to focus your attention on this factor. Review all suggested steps and ideas. Ask yourself: "What have we truly already implemented?" In this situation, the checklist at the end of each chapter on each of the quality characteristics will prove especially helpful.

No Change of the Minimum Factor

- *Are you again focusing on a quality factor that you had previously worked on, after having worked on other quality factors in the meantime?* This case usually only occurs in a church that has already used the church profile tool for some time. Maybe you had "passionate spirituality" as your minimum factor four years ago. You improved it successfully. Then you addressed the factors "functional structures" and "loving relationships." But now "passionate spirituality" has surfaced again as the minimum factor. This history will influence your way of dealing with the ideas in this book. Maybe some of the steps taken previously have been forgotten now and need to be revived. Or perhaps your constituency has changed in the meantime so much that it is useful to repeat the same steps as previously, but now with different participants.

"A Second Round"—focusing on a Minimum Factor That Has Been Dealt with Earlier

- *Are you dealing with a large church or with a small one?* It makes a world of difference if you are working with a minimum factor in a 1000-member church or in a small church with about 30 people in attendance. The size of your church is an important factor that needs to influence your choice of steps to be taken. The leadership structure, processes of decision making, available workers, communication pathways, rooms, financial resources and many other factors differ considerably in churches of different size.

Church Size

- *How many supportive resources for natural church development are already available in your country?* Our institute is developing resources for each of the eight quality characteristics to support churches in their endeavor to apply natural church development principles. At this time (Spring 1998), there are six of the eight

Availability of Materials

building blocks available in the German language; in English the first three resources will become available later this year (1998). Other language materials are developed at different speeds. But you do not have to wait to get to work just because certain materials are not yet available in your context. You may have to modify certain ideas and steps. You may know other resources that, while not developed on the basis of natural church development concepts, may—with some modifications—help you in your task to improve your minimum factor. You may also know some resources offered by your denomination or church organization which may not communicate universally applicable principles, but which may fit your situation quite well.

Individualize Ideas

In short: The ideas in the following pages offer you some guidelines you can use to set your own qualitative goals (see page 29). The help of an outside consultant (a church growth consultant, coach, trainer, etc.) may be very useful at this stage. It is not the job of a church consultant to bombard a church with smart advice ("You have to do it now this way or that way . . ."), rather to help Christians in their own situation to develop a church growth program which fits their church.

For each of the eight quality characteristics the following pages offer four building blocks:

Test Question

- Instead of a definition of each of the quality characteristics, you will find a box with a short question whose answer will sensitize you to the actual condition of your church in this area. Below the question there are references to additional information in the book *Natural Church Development*.

Biblical Illustration

- There is another box with the title "Biblical Illustration," where we selected a Bible verse that captures the essence of each of the quality characteristics. But please note that the text is neither intended to furnish a Biblical "proof" for a quality factor, nor "legitimize" it, nor does this text offer the most important insight the Bible has on the subject. It is just a good Biblical illustration, which can be helpful when you are trying to communicate the meaning of a quality factor to other Christians.

Practical Steps

- In the section "Practical Steps" you will find ideas for steps you can take in your own situation. But in each case you are invited to *adapt* the idea to your church. It is possible that a suggested activity triggers a totally new idea in your mind about how a principle could be put into practice. You will have to select those suggestions which best fit the situation in your church. It is important to make your selection aimed at a quality-oriented goal (see page 29).

Checklist

- Checklists can be used at any time during the church development process, even if the quality factor in question is not your current minimum factor. Simply check off those points that already describe your church. At each point checked you are asked to indicate in what ways this measure has already been implemented. You may come to the conclusion that, in your situation, the suggested measure should not be realized—neither at this time nor in the future. *In this case it is imperative to write down how it would be advantageous for the growth of the church not to realize the suggested measure.* This step will protect you from rejecting proposed measures just because they seem unpleasant or unusual. If you decide against a suggested measure you should have good reasons, namely benefits for the growth of the church.

Not All at Once

Finally, do not be discouraged when at first you can only check a few points in the lists. Maybe the timing for some of the suggested steps is not yet right. It might be better to do them a year later. The function of these checklists is to help you keep certain points in mind, even though you might not be able to work on them just now. The more you make progress in the process of church development the more checks you should appear on your checklists.

Worksheet: Conditions in the Church

Review again the description of the different starting situations of churches on pages 43-44. Then jot down your observations about the current conditions of your church and what consequences this would have for your work on improving the quality of the minimum factor. This step will help you to select those measures among the ones suggested which will fit your situation best.

1. Minimum factor score:

Consequences?

2. Type of church:

Consequences?

3. Prior experience in natural church development:

Consequences?

4. No change in previously identified minimum factor:

Consequences?

5. "Second round" for previously worked on minimum factor:

Consequences?

6. Church size:

Consequences?

7. Availability of work resources:

Consequences?

Quality Characteristic 1: Empowering Leadership

Test Question: Is the ministry of the leaders focusing on equipping other Christians to serve? See NCD, pages 34-35

If this quality characteristic is the minimum factor of your church, you will only be able to make progress as your church leaders are willing to work on themselves and their leadership style. If this is the case, there is no other minimum factor where such rapid progress can be made in a relatively short time frame. In contrast to the other seven quality characteristics, which deal mostly with change processes that involve the whole church, this factor usually relates to a relatively small group of people.

"This quality characteristic is one of those factors plagued with the most anxieties and taboos."

Our experiences indicate that this quality characteristic is one of those vexed with the greatest number of anxieties and taboos: "Hopefully this will not be our minimum factor!" These anxieties are often based on a misunderstanding of the minimum factor strategy which does not necessarily proclaim that the church is especially defective in this area. It only indicates an area where invested energies will bring probably the greatest results for the growth of the church.

Interestingly enough, "empowering leadership" is a relatively frequent minimum factor, particularly in growing churches with a high quality index. The reason for this is that in rapidly

Biblical Motto: ". . . to prepare God's people for works of service, so that the body of Christ may be built up."
Ephesians 4:12

growing churches, the standards expected of leaders increase enormously. It makes sense therefore to invest extra great energies into the leadership factor. The expectations for "empowering leaders" change rapidly in growing churches.

 ## Your Thoughts:

Please indicate here which of the following practical ideas are most relevant for the situation of your church:

Practical Steps

"Empowering leaders are themselves dependent on being empowered."

Remember that empowering leaders are themselves dependent upon being empowered continually.

Every leader that invests himself into other people needs mentors who invest themselves into him or her. Mentoring can happen through official as well as informal relationships. The more extensive their responsibility as leaders, the more they need people in their lives who are interested in their spiritual growth, and in bringing out more and more of that potential that God has put into them. Only the person who has experienced the beneficial impact of such processes can help others experience the same.

* *Do the leaders in your church have mentors who care about their spiritual growth? Who would be able to do such a ministry?*

_____

_____

Take Advantage of Consultants

Look for an external ally

You will experience great help by asking an external consultant to accompany your work as a leadership team. You can discuss with him questions of how to apply general principles of growth in the specific context of your church. He can resource you with help that is tailored to your situation. In the meantime, there are consultants who have been trained according to the principles of natural church development and are experienced in its processes. Through the address on the information sheet that comes with the questionnaires, you can find out about consultants in your area.

* *The following persons would be possible external consultants:*

_____

_____

Recognize Your Giftedness and Limitations

Find out in which areas God has gifted you as a leader and in which areas you are not gifted.

Just like other Christians, God has gifted the leaders in the church with specific gifts—and not with many other gifts. Even a pastor does not have to become an "egg-laying, wool-milk-pig" that is, a super gifted person, because this is not part of God's plan. When such unrealistic expectations are projected onto leaders, they must resist them decisively. For this reason it is very important that you have a clear sense of your own gifts and limitations. Since one of your primary responsibilities is to help people find a spot in the ministry of the church that matches their gifts, it is important that you live this principle first.

- *As a leadership team find out about your own gifts ("The Three Colors of Ministry" that contains "The Gift Test," might be helpful; it has the advantage of being compatible with other resources for natural church development). After identifying the gifts, list those which are strongly represented in your leadership team.*

Let the gifts of your team complement your own.

Allow Yourself to Be Complemented

Let's say a leader finds out that God has not given him or her a well-developed giftedness in administration. This insight underlines the urgent need for people who can complement him or her in this area. Maybe a leader senses that his strength is not the ability to strike up a conversation with unchurched people about questions of faith. This awareness should motivate leaders to identify those in the church to whom God has indeed given the gift of evangelism. God has not given one Christian all the gifts, but every Christian some of the gifts necessary to build up the body of Christ. The more you use your own gift, you will become aware of just how much you need the ministry of others to complement your own one-sidedness. This is the reason why it is so important to help every member of the church discover their spiritual gifts and use them to build up the church. As you use the resources above, you can find out which gifts God has placed among your team members.

- *List here those gifts that are not strongly represented in your leadership team. It is in these areas that complementary gifts of others are especially needed.*

- *Write down how you want to help your coworkers in the church to identify their gifts:*

Define Your Goals *As a leadership team, define qualitative goals for the development of the church.*

Empowering leadership must focus on clear goals. You should be able to describe in precise terms which goals you will focus your energies on in the immediate future. If you do not accomplish many other things in the future, you don't have to become disturbed as long as you are devoting a good part of your efforts to those goals you have set for yourself. Such goals should be written down. Writing them down brings clarity of thought. Make sure that your goals can be evaluated. "We want to work towards reaching more and more people with our group studies" is a good declaration of intention, but not a goal. A clearly stated goal would be: "By April of next year, we will have organized two new small groups whose leaders have been trained to apply the principle of multiplication in their work." Another goal would be: "As of next June, the quality factor 'empowering leadership' will no longer be the minimum factor of our church."

- *Within the next six months (date:_____) the following goals will be reached:*

_____

_____

_____

_____

_____

_____

_____

Reduce Activities *Reduce the number of your activities.*

This is an extraordinarily important point. It is a misunderstanding to think that in church growth, the goal is to increase the number of activities and with it the investment of energy without limits. If you want to embark on new things, you have to let go of old activities. The principles of natural church development will help you to develop a wise outlook for those measures which aim to bring about great results for the kingdom of God with relatively little energy investment. The important thing is that the leader is capable of selecting and concentrating on those things that make a difference based on his or her schedule. Therefore, eliminate, as much as possible, those activities that do not contribute directly to church development.

- *We will eliminate the following activities by (date)_____ from our program:*

_____

_____

As a leadership team, conduct the training program "Learning to Think Biotically."

Practicing Biotic Thinking

This training program, found on pages 123 to 191, is not necessarily important or even recommended for every Christian in your church. But those who are bearing leadership responsibilities in the church should really make an effort to master the biotic principles of church development. The purpose of the program is to "play through" and practice biotic (in contrast to spiritualizing or technocratic) decision making for those future critical issues that will make a difference for your church. Those who go through this training will develop a greater sensitivity for the principle of spiritual self-organization.

- *By (date)_____ our leadership team will have worked through the training program.*

_____

_____

_____

_____

Invest Yourself into a Selected Few Co-workers

Invest in Few People

Just as the task of the pastor cannot be to care for all church members in the same way (according to the model of the "pastor-church") we should not expect every volunteer leader to do all the necessary tasks of their ministry by themselves. Rather, you should invest your energies primarily in equipping a selected few of your leaders, who then invest their efforts into other Christians. This dynamic makes the ongoing "multiplication" (the second biotic principle) possible. The goal must be to constantly select new emerging leaders, then prepare them to develop their leadership potential, so that after some time, they can carry out ministry tasks on their own.

- *During the next six months we will work intensively with the following Christians who exhibit the potential for leadership:*

_____

_____

• *We will take the following steps to help emerging leaders to develop their God-given potential and participate responsibly in the work of the church:*

_____

_____

Monitor Your Effectiveness

Monitor the effectiveness of your steps.

In order to monitor how effective your steps have been, you should conduct a new church profile after about six months. In this way, you can determine if you need to continue your efforts in the area of "empowering leadership," or if your efforts have been so successful that you should move on to the next quality characteristic (your new minimum factor).

We will do a new church profile to Monitor our progress on _____ (date).

_____

_____

Checklist:
Empowering Leadership

❏ The leaders of our church will meet at least once a quarter with a church consultant/trainer/coach to focus on goals and plans for church development.

With whom?

❏ We have developed a coaching structure for the leaders in the different ministry areas of our church.

What does it look like?

❏ The leaders meet with their coaches at least once a quarter.

When was the last meeting?

❏ Pastors and church leaders have discovered their spiritual gifts and know which tasks fit their giftedness.

Examples?

❏ The members of the church leadership team have passed on to others those tasks that do not fit their own gifts.

Which ones?

❏ The pastor has found members with the gift of helps to unburden him or her in different areas.

Whom?

❏ The church leadership team has a plan to help every Christian find a place in the ministry of the church that fits his or her gifts.

What does it look like?

❏ Church leadership has developed short-, medium-, and long-term objectives for church development.

Examples?

❏ People active in a ministry of the church have actually participated in defining these objectives.

In what ways?

❏ The leaders of the church have formulated a personal growth plan for themselves that describes how they want to grow in faith.

What does this plan look like?

❏ The pastor spends much time in prayer to receive a vision from God for his personal life and for the church.

How much?

❏ The pastor invests himself/herself into 3-4 members with the gift of leadership by meeting with them on a regular basis to further their growth.

In whom?

❏ We regularly, critically evaluate activities and programs in our church.

When was the last time?

❏ Our church leadership team has identified the needs of our members with the help of intentional conversations and surveys.

Result?

❏ We have discovered ways to apply the existing strengths of our church to develop the quality factor of "empowering leadership."

Which strengths?

❏ We have identified some barriers that seem to block the successful implementation of needed practical steps, and we have met them in appropriate ways.

Examples?

❏ The results of our measures for improvement are monitored regularly.

When was this done last?

❏ The steps we are taking are evaluated according to biotic principles.

With what results?

❏ We have set a date for a new church profile.

When?

Other:

Quality Characteristic 2: Gift-Oriented Ministry

Test Question: Are the tasks in the church distributed according to the criterion of the spiritual gifts of individual Christians?

See NCD, pages 24-25

If your church finds this quality characteristic as its minimum factor, it does not mean that your workers are doing "bad" work. Rather, it indicates that the work in your church is not gift-oriented enough. This situation is one of the most frequent causes for the enormous work overload of volunteers, especially of the most engaged of your members.

"Nowhere can you study better than here what it means to develop the church according to God's plan."

As you work through the practical ideas for the other seven quality characteristics, you will notice that the concept of spiritual gifts plays a central role in all of them. What is at stake here is nothing less than the very character of the "body of Christ": Every Christian is a member of this body, and the gifts each one has received will determine the role he or she is to play in that body according to God's will (*Natural Church Development*, page 117). In other words, if members do not discover and use their spiritual gifts, a church cannot expect great progress in any area of church development. Moreover, there is no area where you can better study the difference between technocratic growth programs that have been invented by humans, and church development according to God's plan, than in this area.

 Your Thoughts:

Please indicate here which of the following practical ideas are most relevant for the situation of your church:

Biblical Motto: "Each one should use whatever gift he has received to serve others, faithfully administering God's grace in its various forms."

1 Peter 4:10

Practical Steps

"Church development means: Every Christian serving at the place where God has called him or her to be."

Through sermons, Bible studies, seminars, etc., create understanding for the subject of "gift-oriented ministry."

Despite the fact that the concept of "gift-oriented ministry" is extraordinarily powerful for the development of the church it is one of the least consistently practiced concepts. Ultimately, church development does not mean anything else but helping Christians to find the place in the church where God has called them to serve. When there is progress in this area, the church experiences the body of Christ functioning according to God's plan. In this way many things almost regulate themselves. If the principle of "gift-oriented ministry" is to significantly shape the everyday life of the church, it is important to inform people about it at different levels in different ways, through sermons, Bible studies, seminars, etc.

- *In the next six months we will use the following means to help the members of the church to better understand the concept of "gift-oriented ministry":*

_____

_____

_____

Start a Discovery Process

Help all Christians to discover their gifts.

It is critical not to stop at the mere communication of information. Instead, help church members in concrete ways to identify their spiritual gifts. There are several resources which have been developed that can help all Christians discover their gifts. We recommend the workbook "The Three Colors of Ministry" that contains "The Gift Test". We have developed this resource especially for churches using the principles of natural church development. (English edition projected to be available: Late 2001) The person who works through this workbook is led to a clear understanding of those areas he or she has been gifted for by God. If you already have a well functioning small group ministry, you can use these workbooks in your small groups. Groups that have gone through this process represent an enormous potential for future church development.

- *In the following ways we will make sure that every Christian will discover his or her spiritual gifts during the next six months:*

_____

_____

Collect and assess the results of the gift test.

Some churches have gone through the first two steps only to wonder why they have not seen anything happening. Church leadership must receive the result of the gift tests to enable them to align future ministry with the rightly gifted people God has already given to the church. Leaders should insist on being informed about the results of everyone who has completed the gift test. Then you should record the results in a master list and assess the strength of the different (manifest and latent) gifts in your church. Such a summary perspective will give you special insights into the specific calling of your church.

- *By (date) _____ we will have evaluated the results of the gift test for the whole church.*

Train Gift Counselors.

Now comes the exciting part. Schedule a meeting with every member who has discovered his or her spiritual gifts to discuss their personal calling. During this conversation, the results of the gift test can be evaluated while addressing other factors that go beyond the question of giftedness, such as family situation, time restrictions, personality structure, preferences, and training. This conversation should be conducted by workers that have been prepared and trained specifically for this ministry. You will discover that this task is not very complicated—if one has been prepared carefully.

- *In the following ways we will prepare one (for a very small church) or more gift counselors:*

_____

_____

Offer continuous gift counseling.

Gift counseling must go beyond just a single event, becoming a "fixed institution" in the church. Every new Christian and each new worker should be able to profit from this ministry. During the meetings, you will see that some Christians are quite clearly at the place where God has called them to be, while others are not. It is important that leaders help these persons to find a place in the church that corresponds to their gifts and thus their calling. During the gift counseling session, a written ministry description is developed for every Christian.

- *The first round of gift counseling meetings will be completed by (date) _____. Each task in the church should have a written job description.*

Reduce the Number of Duties

Cut those tasks that do not contribute to the growth of the church.

In many cases, the concept of "gift-oriented ministry" does not bear fruit because the members are burdened with so many tasks that are not wrong, but do not bear much fruit for the growth of the church. In natural church development, the goal is not to increase the number of activities as much as possible, but rather to concentrate on key activities. If many of your workers in the church are already overwhelmed with responsibilities, we recommend you cut as many activities as possible from the total church program. Churches that approach this decision radically are often amazed how many tasks can be dropped and how many new energies can be freed for church development.

- *The following responsibilities can be dropped in our church:*

_____

_____

_____

_____

_____

Encourage Your Evangelists

Make sure to involve those with the gift of evangelism in evangelistic ministries.

Be sure to identify those Christians to whom God has given the gift of evangelism. During our weekend seminars where we use the gift test, we have found no exception to C. Peter Wagner's thesis, "that God has given the gift of evangelism to about 10 percent of all Christians." Church leaders must know these persons. Make sure they invest all their energies in evangelism, even if that means that they have to be relieved of other responsibilities. Help them devote themselves on a continuous basis to active evangelistic ministry. If every Christian whom God has given the gift of evangelism helps two people per year to come to faith in Christ (a goal which is realistic for people with the gift of evangelism), by their ministry alone, the number of Christians would double in just four years!

- *The following Christians in our church have the gift of evangelism:*

_____

_____

_____

- *By (date) _____ we will have talked with each one of them to help them concentrate more intentionally on evangelistic ministry than previously.*

Monitor the effectiveness of your steps.

Monitor Your Effectiveness

In order to monitor how effective your steps have been, you should conduct a new church profile after about six months. In this way you can examine your need to continue your efforts in the area of this quality factor "gift-oriented ministry," or discover that your efforts have been so successful that you can move on to the next quality characteristic (your new minimum factor).

We will do a new church profile to monitor our progress on _____ (date).

Checklist: Gift-Oriented Ministry

❏ Our church continuously teaches about spiritual gifts and their use in our church.

How?

❏ At least 75 percent of our small groups have dealt substantially with the question of spiritual gifts.

In what ways?

❏ At least 75 percent of those attending the worship service have discovered their spiritual gifts.

How?

❏ At least 75 percent of those Christians who have discovered their gifts are also involved in a ministry in the church that fits their giftedness.

Who makes sure it is so?

❏ We have a master list that indicates how the gifts are distributed in the church.

Where?

❏ We encourage people to get out of responsibilities that do not correspond with their gifts.

When was the last time?

❏ For most of the current and future responsibilities in the church we have written job descriptions.

Where can they be found?

❏ We have people in the church whose main responsibility consists of coordinating the match between gifts and tasks in the church (gift counselors).

Names?

❏ The gift counselor(s) in our church have the necessary resources to support them in their ministry.

Which ones?

❏ We have had at least one conversation with each Christian who has discovered his gifts about his calling.

With whom?

❏ Those who have received the gift of evangelism by God are cared for by one of our workers continuously.

By whom?

❏ Every person who joins the church receives help in discovering his gifts and using them to the glory of God.

Who cares for this ministry?

❏ Christians continually testify during church services how God blesses the use of spiritual gifts.

When was the last time?

❏ The pastor(s) of the church is (are) concentrating on responsibilities for which God has indeed gifted them.

For instance?

❏ There are possibilities for experimenting in ministry in each area of giftedness in our church.

Examples?

❏ In our church, there is a climate open to experimentation.

How is it encouraged?

❏ Our church offers training and leadership opportunities for different areas of giftedness.

Which?

❏ Each volunteer worker in the church has a supervisor that provides continuous coaching.

Names of these supervisors?

❏ Many of the gifts in this church are consciously linked to ministries for people who are not Christians.

Examples?

❏ We encourage Christians to periodically test their gifts anew.

In what ways?

❏ Church members are also helped to experience growth in the fruit of the Spirit (Galatians 5:22).

How?

❏ We have discovered ways to apply the existing strengths of our church to develop the quality factor "gift-oriented ministry."

Which strengths?

❏ We have identified some barriers that seem to block the successful implementation of needed practical steps and we have met them in appropriate ways.

Examples?

❏ The results of our measures for improvement are monitored regularly.

When was this done last?

❏ The steps we are taking are evaluated according to biotic principles.

With what results?

❏ We have set a date for a new church profile.

When?

Other:

Quality Characteristic 3: Passionate Spirituality

Test Question: Is the spiritual life of the members characterized by prayer, enthusiasm and boldness?

See NCD, pages 26-27

One of the interesting findings of our research indicates that the secret of growing churches is definitely not found in their particular style of spirituality (charismatic, non-charismatic, liturgical, or non-liturgical, etc.), but in the level of passion at which faith is lived out among its members. Admittedly, some styles of spirituality have more "built-in" affinity with spiritual passion than others. But passion in the spiritual life can be expressed in the context of the most varied forms of piety. Moreover, the level of spirituality can be intensified in any context.

"This quality characteristic is not about promoting a specific style of spirituality."

The following practical suggestions are not designed to win you over to a specific style of spirituality. How you will apply these ideas depends in large measure on the characteristics of your church. No matter what your preferred spiritual styles are, this quality factor deals with the question of how to make the Christian faith the holistic experience of a personal encounter with Christ—and this always includes our senses. Without this personal relationship with Christ, there are no "styles of spirituality" that merit this designation. Wherever the personal relationship with Christ is intensified we discover that passionate spirituality is freed up seemingly "all by itself."

Biblical Motto: *"Never be lacking in zeal, but keep your spiritual fervor, serving the Lord. Be joyful in hope, patient in affliction, faithful in prayer."* Romans 12:11-12

 Your Thoughts:

Please indicate here which of the following practical ideas are most relevant for the situation of your church:

Practical Steps

"As a leader, are you curious to learn something new from God, or has much of your ministry become a dull routine?"

Be aware of the imitation modeling function of leaders.

The unquestionable prerequisite of passionate spirituality in the church is the passion that characterizes the life of its leaders. Are you yourself curious to learn something new from God? Do you have a strong expectancy that God will "show up" in your church and do a miracle? Or has much of what you do become sheer humdrum? As Christians with leadership responsibility in the church, we should block out at least two consecutive days devoted to prayer and fasting. Ask God for a new vision for the church. Ask Him to increase your own faith. Ask Him that your future work in the church be increasingly filled with joy. But above all, ask Him to show you those top priorities that are crucial for the growth of the church.

• *I will devote the following days with the following leaders of our church totally to prayer and silence before God:*

_____

_____

_____

_____

Integrate the Gifts

Make sure that your members are involved based on their spiritual gifts.

Our experience shows that the concept of "gift-oriented ministry" greatly affects passion in the spiritual life. According to a survey of the users of *The Gift Test*, 51 percent said that as a result of utilizing the gift test, they are "happier than before." This comes as no surprise: A Christian who serves God in the area of his or her giftedness and calling will be able to fulfill his responsibilities with much more enthusiasm than somebody who is just doing his duty. For many Christians, the discovery of their gifts has become a key experience in their spiritual existence. Thus they received a new, God-given, spiritual consciousness that has affected all the areas of their lives in a positive way.

This is why one of a church leaders top priorities must be to ensure that all Christians discover their spiritual gifts and get involved in a ministry that fits their giftedness. For information about resources for this purpose, please refer to the chapter on "gift-oriented ministry" (pages 55-62).

• *By (date)* _____ *we will take the following steps to help church members discover their spiritual gifts and the place in the church that corresponds to their gifts:*

_____

_____

_____

_____

Identify those Christians God has given the gift of praying.

Recruit Prayer Partners

A beautiful "side effect" of the process of identifying the gifts in your church is the discovery of members to whom God has given the gift of prayer. These Christians have a key role in the work of this minimum factor. These are people who love to intercede over prolonged periods of time for certain concerns, and in the process, have experiences of how God actually answers their prayers. Persons with this gift must have enough time to actually exercise this gift (you may have to let them drop other responsibilities in the church if necessary). Make sure they regularly receive prayer requests from other church members. Finally, increase the opportunities where they can share about their prayer ministry during church programs such as the worship service.

• *The following persons in our church have the gift of prayer:*

_____

_____

_____

_____

_____

Train Christians with the gift of counseling for their ministry.

Train Lay Counselors

The gift of counseling is another spiritual gift that can significantly impact the level of passion in the spiritual life of the church. Our research found that this is actually one of the most widespread gifts in the body of Christ. The problem however, is that many Christians have not yet discovered their giftedness in this area, and consequently are using this gift only in fragmented ways. As you use the gift test in your church, you will become aware of Christians to whom God has given the gift of counseling. It is critical that they be trained for continuous pastoral ministry (either by competent guest trainers, or in courses outside of the church). Pastoral care is not a ministry that can be left solely to the pastor or to full-time staff people. Instead you must create an infra structure that makes it more feasible for Christians to care for one another.

• During the next six months we plan the following training events for lay counselors:

_____

_____

_____

Offer Training in Praying

Recruit the small groups in your church for a multi-week training course in praying.

"The Three Colors of Spirituality" is not yet available in English. (Please call for other suggestions.) There are many good books on the subject of prayer. Most of them, however, overemphasize one certain aspect of prayer which the author has discovered as being important. Our training course tries to learn from all these perspectives, and integrate them into a process that helps every Christian to develop his or her own "prayer profile." The purpose of the program is not to duplicate specific forms of praying, but to practice the kind of personal relationship with God that fits the personality of each individual Christian. This prayer training course also incorporates additional principles of a passionate yet down-to-earth spirituality which is often overlooked in Christian circles.

• The following small groups should use the training program "Learning to Be Passionate":

_____

_____

_____

Find those factors that block spiritual passion in your church.

Identify Passion Killers

Most churches have, over time, unconsciously developed a multitude of mechanisms that block spiritual passion. Here is a list of the most frequent passion killers that we have identified in churches we worked with. Each passion killer has, interestingly, a positive and intelligible origin. What we are concerned about is not this "true kernel", but rather the negative effects on our churches:

1. *Puritanism:* A reaction against the "I'll-do-it-if-I-like-it Christianity" with the motto: "no images, no art, no cultural activities, no music, fast rather than feast." Christians influenced by Puritan values view growth in faith as a process of becoming more and more aloof to "external things."

2. *Animosity against institutions:* Many Christians support the thought of discovering spiritual gifts, and giving more prominence to prayer in the church; but according to their opinion, this has to be a spontaneous process and should never be planned.

3. *Righteousness by works:* Legalistic tendencies in various forms that always build on the premise that we have to "earn heaven."

4. *Fatalism:* The belief in fate is typical for many non-Christian religions but has intruded into Christianity as well. It centers in the thought that everything we experience is God-sent. Therefore we need to submit to our fate, whether good or bad, in order to stay in harmony with the God of our fate.

5. *Feelings of inferiority:* Some groups implicitly or expressly communicate the attitude: "Whatever you do is an expression of sin." This attitude makes it nearly impossible to ever enjoy the Christian faith.

6. *Whimsical pleasure:* Many mistake a whimsical pleasure principle with spiritual passion. Thus, leaders don't dare to ask for binding commitments because they fear this could be demanding too much. What they overlook is this: It is in dedicated and committed service to others that we find one of the most powerful sources of happiness in life.

7. *Magical expectations:* A widespread attitude hidden behind some seemingly pious faith practices is expressed in the motto: "If you do this or that just right, you will surely get this result."

8. *Ecstasy dependency:* There is a danger in a kind of "conference Christianity" that feeds off one extraordinary experience which can only be surpassed by the next one. Those who focus on these kinds of events may become blind to the everyday and down-to-earth principles which are the soil that feeds spiritual passion in the life of the church.

• *Consider the "passion killers" mentioned above and ask yourself: How strong is each one of these factors in our church? Indicate your evaluation on a scale from 1 to 10 (1 = very weak; 10 = very strong). As a second step ask yourself: What could we do to overcome those passion killers that are represented the strongest?*

1. Puritanism   1 – 2 – 3 – 4 – 5 – 6 – 7 – 8 – 9 – 10

2. Anti-institutionalism   1 – 2 – 3 – 4 – 5 – 6 – 7 – 8 – 9 – 10

3. Righteousness by works   1 – 2 – 3 – 4 – 5 – 6 – 7 – 8 – 9 – 10

4. Fatalism   1 – 2 – 3 – 4 – 5 – 6 – 7 – 8 – 9 – 10

5. Inferior feelings   1 – 2 – 3 – 4 – 5 – 6 – 7 – 8 – 9 – 10

6. Whimsical pleasure   1 – 2 – 3 – 4 – 5 – 6 – 7 – 8 – 9 – 10

7. Magical expectations   1 – 2 – 3 – 4 – 5 – 6 – 7 – 8 – 9 – 10

8. Ecstasy dependency   1 – 2 – 3 – 4 – 5 – 6 – 7 – 8 – 9 – 10

Develop a Culture of Appreciation

Avoid appeals to the guilty conscience.

One of the most dangerous traps for leaders who want to enhance the growth of their church is the temptation to get the right things accomplished in the wrong ways: They attempt to motivate Christians by causing feelings of guilt. While some people can be motivated by guilt in the short run for certain projects, in the long run, the consequences of this approach are mostly counterproductive. Instead, work to develop a "culture of appreciation" in your church. Be a good model by continuously expressing your appreciation when your members have accomplished something good. If the entire work of the church is not built on a positive spirit, passionate spirituality will not make progress.

• *In the left column write the names of some of your members and in the right column those things they have done well during the last few weeks. When was the last time they have received any praise and recognition for it?*

Name of the member   **What was done well?**

_____   _____

_____   _____

_____   _____

_____   _____

_____   _____

_____   _____

_____   _____

_____   _____

_____   _____

_____   _____

• *Make sure these persons are recognized privately and in public.*

Monitor External Factors

Monitor all events and programs in your church in view of their positive atmosphere.

In your situation, external factors (such as . . . condition of the room, the way people greet one another, atmosphere, etc.) deserve specific attention. These are all factors that "preach along" as the Word of God is communicated. Is the Christian's spiritual life to be filled in the long term with passion instead of being considered a troublesome duty, it is important that this passion becomes tangible for all five senses.

- *Look at the programs and activities of your church and ask: How could the atmosphere become more friendly/loving/positive?*

Activity/Program

How could the atmosphere be improved?

_____	_____
_____	_____
_____	_____
_____	_____
_____	_____
_____	_____
_____	_____
_____	_____

Monitor Your Effectiveness

Monitor the effectiveness of your steps.

In order to monitor how effective your steps have been, you should conduct a new church profile after about six months. In this way you can examine if you need to continue your efforts in this quality factor, "passionate spirituality", or if your efforts have been so successful that you should move on to the next quality characteristic (your new minimum factor).

We will do a new church profile to monitor our progress on _____ (date).

Checklist: Passionate Spirituality

❑ The pastor and those involved in ministry in our church have developed a plan how to intensify their personal prayer life?

What does it look like?

❑ At least two times a year the pastor spends a whole day to seek God in prayer and listen to His guidance.

When was this done last?

❑ The meaning of prayer is often illustrated by practical examples during the sermons.

When did this occur the last time?

❑ Church members are encouraged to share persoanl experiences with God during the worship service and in the small groups.

When last?

❑ Our leadership team meets regularly for prayer.

When was the last time?

❑ 75 percent of those attending worship are involved in a ministry that corresponds to their spiritual gifts.

How has this been checked?

❑ A regular prayer ministry has been started in our church.

What does it look like?

❑ We have identified all Christians with the gift of praying.

Names?

❑ We have developed concrete possibilities for Christians with this gift to get involved in the ministry of our church.

Which possiblities?

❑ Christians with the gift of prayer are continually suplied with prayer requests of the church.

Who is organizing this?

❑ We have identified Christians with the gift of counseling.

Names?

❑ We have helped Christians with the gift of counseling to get involved in appropriate ministries.

Which ministries?

❏ We have started a prayer team which is praying for the pastor and the church.

When and where?

❏ Together with the leadership team of the church the pastor has formulated faith goals for our church.

What do they look like?

❏ In sermons and in the small groups the significance of the Bible for our daily life is often discussed.

Examples?

❏ Our small groups offer concrete helps for applying principles of God's Word in everyday living.

Examples?

❏ We have created programs that deal with learning the fundamentals of faith (prayer, Bible reading, etc.)

Which?

❏ In our church we encourage and support prayer partnerships.

In what ways?

❏ We constantly further a climate of creativity and experimentation in our church.

How?

❏ All the programs, ministries and activities of our church have been evaluated in view of their positive atmosphere and corrective steps have been taken where appropriate.

Which corrective steps?

❏ We have discovered ways to use the existing strengths of our church to improve the quality factor "passionate spirituality."

Which strengths?

❏ We have identified some barriers that seem to block the successful implementation of needed practical steps and we have dealt with them in appropriate ways.

Examples?

❏ The results of our measures for improvement in this area are monitored regularly.

When was this done last?

❏ The steps we are taking are evaluated according to biotic principles.

With what results?

❏ We have set a date for a new church profile.

When?

❏ Other:

Quality Characteristic 4: Functional Structures

"There are no "off-the rack" functional structures.

If the quality characteristic, "functional structures", is the minimum factor of your church, it can have extremely variable cases. Often churches have to keep in mind a multitude of complex forms and regulations which may have been useful at the time they were instituted, but which lost their functionality over

Test Question: Are the forms, regulations, and institutions of the church designed according to the criterion of what is demonstrably the most useful for the development of the church here and now? See NCD, pages 28-29

time. In other situations—as in the case of a new church planting project— this quality characteristic emerges as the minimum factor because there are simply not enough structures formed yet.

Already these two examples reveal that the practical steps that need to be taken to improve this factor will vary considerably depending on the actual point of departure. Thus your church must discover its own solution of what functional structures will look like in your context. There are no "off-the-rack" functional structures.

Biblical Motto: "The Sabbath was made for men, not man for the Sabbath." Mark 2:27

Your Thoughts:

Please indicate here which of the following practical ideas are most relevant for the situation of your church:

Practical Steps

Develop a stronger awareness in your church that the question of structures has spiritual relevance.

"The counter-productive paradigms that characterize Christianity have clearly left their own footprints here."

Our research indicates that in many groups which are spiritually motivated, the issue of functional structures is not taken seriously enough. Two extremes are especially detrimental to the growth of the church: first, a "morphological fundamentalism" (motto: "The structures here cannot be changed!"); second, an a-historical "spiritualism" (motto: "Structures are irrelevant for spiritual processes!") In the first case the term "functional" creates resistance; in the second it is the term "structures" itself that is the irritant. Thus the counter-productive paradigms that characterize Christianity have clearly left their own footprints here.

In your situation, it is important to be aware that the question of functional structures is not at all a secondary matter, but has important spiritual significance. The goal is to increasingly develop structures in the church that can undergird the process of church development as strongly as possible.

• *Does your church tend more towards a technocratic understanding (e.g.: static approach to structures, traditionalism, morphological fundamentalism, conservatism) or to a spiritualizing understanding of structures (structures are not important, spiritually irrelevant, an expression of the illusion that growth can be manufactured)?*

❏ Rather technocratic

❏ Rather spiritualistic

❏ A mix of both

• *What concrete steps could you take to increase the awareness in your church of the spiritual significance of functional structures?*

_____

_____

_____

_____

_____

_____

_____

Take Responsibility

Take full responsibility for the structures that currently can be found in your church.

There is hardly any other area in the life of a church where responsibility so often tends to be shoved on "others" as in the area of church structures. Few leaders see this as something that needs to be developed by practical measures, and with much innovation and creativity. All church structures have been invented (sometimes a long time ago) by humans and can consequently only be changed by people. If somebody is new on the church leadership team, it is very possible that he or she has not personally contributed to the genesis of these structures. Yet in each church, it is the leadership team that bears full responsibility for the current structures. Leaders that shove this responsibility on "the tradition" or "past generations" or "the circumstances" use the same mechanism that has had such troubling consequences in all areas of life ever since Adam ("Eve gave me the fruit") and Eve ("It's the serpent's fault!"). The shirking of personal responsibility is often framed in deep religiosity ("respect of tradition").

• *If the problem described here applies also to your church leadership, it can be helpful to illustrate the foundational problem—the shirking of responsibility—with examples that do not have anything to do with the question of structures. The transfer of insights to the question of church structures should be realized as far as possible by each person who has a leadership responsibility in the church. Write down what could be done to facilitate these processes.*

_____

_____

_____

_____

_____

_____

Define your church mission statement in writing.

Prepare a Church Mission Statement

Each church has a certain calling, a God-given individuality. To have a standard you can use to evaluate existing structures, it is important to concretize this individuality by writing a church mission statement. If you have already developed such a mission statement some time ago, you should ask yourself now again: What makes us distinct? What three adjectives best describe the character of our church? What kind of persons feel especially at home in our church? If you have never asked these questions you should ask them now.

As you proceed to develop a church mission statement, you should pay attention to the following points:

a. It is absolutely necessary to formulate your church mission statement in writing. It forces you to be precise. It should be short—35 words are enough. Avoid clichés and filler.

b. Don't confuse the church mission statement with a diplomatic paper, in which everybody can find his or her input but which does not communicate anything. Be as specific as possible.

c. Once you have defined a church mission statement, it is open for revision and changes. If God gives you new insights change what you have formulated.

d. Present the church mission statement to the church. Use its text in sermons and church programs. Every church member should know why your church exists.

• *Our church mission statement reads:*

_____

_____

_____

_____

_____

_____

_____

_____

_____

_____

_____

_____

Prepare a Church Mission Statement

Identify enhancing and hindering structures.

In many churches, the problem is that church structures are not clearly identified. They may be the backdrop of every single church decision and thus influence the life of the church, but nobody actually knows the importance of these structures. Therefore, in order to be able to deal with your structures, it is important to actually identify and categorize the growth enhancing and hindering structures of your church.

• *Write down which church forms, institutions, and regulations you believe effectively serve the growth of the church.*

_____

_____

_____

_____

_____

• *Write down which forms/institutions/regulations you believe should be evaluated using church growth effectiveness as a criterion:*

_____

_____

_____

_____

_____

• *Write down which forms/institutions/regulations you regard as unchangeable (denominational policies, etc.):*

_____

_____

_____

_____

_____

Develop a set of measurable goals for the handling of church structures. **Set Reform Goals**

In the light of your church mission statement, you should aim at extending those structures which serve overall goals, while changing or even dismantling those structures that only seem to be a barrier to realizing overall goals. Each church must set its own goals in this process. As you formulate goals, make sure they can be evaluated. For instance: "We want to align our structures more with the will of God" is a good declaration of intention, but not a goal. There is no criterion for evaluation. A goal that can be evaluated would be: "We will have reformed our structures by February of next year in such a way that the quality characteristic "functional structures" is no longer the minimum factor of our church."

• *In view of the change of church structures we set the following goals for the next six months:*

_____

_____

_____

_____

_____

Evaluate all structures according to their potential for multiplication. **Extend the Potential for Multiplication**

There is no one suitable infrastructure for church growth which is generally valid everywhere. What may be right in one situation can be wrong in another. There are, however, generally valid criteria with which any kind of structure can be evaluated. These criteria are described by the six biotic principles. In view of the question of church structures, the principle of "multiplication" has a key function. Evaluate all structures to see how well they promote continuous multiplication or hinder it.

What form could these multiplication structures have? Maybe a few practical examples can stimulate your thoughts. How about the commissioning of department leaders who are responsible for areas of ministry in the church and who are training apprentice leaders? Or implementing training systems that make it a priority for those trained to, in turn, share with others what they have learned. Or a model of evangelism training that instructs brand new believers in evangelism. Or a financial system that operates under the principle that new areas of work must be self-supporting from the beginning. Our goal is not to prescribe any structures. You must develop those forms of structures which have the greatest potential for multiplication in your situation.

• *The following structures must be modified to fit the criterion of multiplication:*

Structure   **Kind of Change**

_____   _____

_____   _____

_____   _____

_____   _____

_____   _____

_____   _____

_____   _____

_____   _____

_____   _____

_____   _____

Make Use of Spiritual Gifts

Apply the existing gifts of your members more consistently to the less developed quality characteristics of your church.

A "functional structure" should make sure that the gifts which God has already given to the church are utilized for the development of the church so that the spiritual harvest is maximized. The New Testament describes the church as the "body of Christ", those Christians who serve God with various gifts as the members of the body. In this picture, the structure of the church can be compared to the central nervous system. Its task is to make sure that the activities of the individual members are coordinated with one another so that the organism can work effectively.

First, all active church members should identify their gifts (see the chapter on "gift-oriented ministry," pages 55-62). When Christians think about which tasks would best fit their giftedness, they should remember to devote the greatest number of gifts possible to those areas of the ministry of the church which, in addition to functional structures, scored the least in the church profile. For instance, if the quality factor "need-oriented evangelism" is relatively weak, relate the gifts of your members especially to the evangelistic work of the church. No matter which gift is identified, evangelism, pastoral care, hospitality, or teaching, think how you can employ them in the area of evangelism.

• *By (date)* _____ *all active members should have discovered their gifts. We will take the following measures to support this process:*

_____

_____

_____

• *The gifts discovered should above all be employed in the following area of church life (write in the quality characteristic that scored lowest besides "functional structures" in the church profile):*

_____

_____

_____

• *The following new ministries/tasks could help us to improve the growth of this quality characteristic.*

_____

_____

_____

• *The following members could have the necessary gifts to take on these ministries/tasks:*

_____

_____

_____

Cut What Is Not Effective

Cut as many programs and activities as possible which do not contribute to the development of the church.

In natural church development the goal is not to increase your energy investment, rather the concentration of energy. This means focusing your existing energies on the most important point. Existing activities and programs have to be evaluated in view of their effective use of the energy which is invested in them. You will usually find many activities that can be cut without affecting the growth of the church adversely. Of course, the challenge of letting ministries which have outlived their usefulness "die a natural death" will often be controversial, but it is a required condition for a healthy growth process. Just as most cells of the human body are renewed over a period of time, so must it happen in the church: old things must die so that new ones can take shape. This is a law that God Himself has embedded in His creation.

• The following activities/groups/programs can be cut in order to free new energies for the development of the church:

_____

_____

_____

Develop an Organizational Chart

Develop and communicate an organizational chart which clearly shows the responsibilities within the church.

Some churches have never developed an organizational chart that shows all the areas of ministry, who is responsible for which area, and who should be contacted when there are problems. Others have developed one before, but have not revised it recently to adjust to current needs. Then there are churches with excellent organizational charts, which are virtually unknown to those in the church. If you are embarking on the task of developing an organizational chart from scratch, you might consider conceptualizing the different areas of ministry in your church, each led by a different leader, by using the eight quality characteristics as your organizing principle. While there is usually someone who is responsible for youth ministry, or public relations, or finances, there is something to be said for having a responsible person for each of the areas of work that are linked to the eight quality characteristics. Finally, the organizational chart should not become a secret document, but must be communicated as broadly as possible.

• By (date) _____ we will have revised our organizational chart thoroughly or developed a new one.

• The new organizational chart will be communicated broadly in the church in the following ways:

_____

_____

_____

_____

Monitor the effectiveness of your steps.

In order to monitor how effective your steps have been you should conduct a new church profile after about six months. This allows you to examine your need to continue your efforts in the area of "functional structures", or if your efforts have been so successful that you should move on to the next quality characteristic (your new minimum factor).

We will do a new church profile to monitor our progress on _____ (date).

_____

_____

Monitor Your Effectiveness

Checklist: Functional Structures

❏ We have critically evaluated all church structures from the perspective of functionality.

When?

❏ Ineffective structures have been discarded or changed.

Which ones?

❏ We have also identified structures which do not currently exist but would be meaningful, and we have prepared concrete plans to introduce those structures.

Which ones?

❏ We have developed a church mission statement and derived concrete action plans.

Which ones?

❏ Our church mission statement is communicated to the church regularly.

When was the last time?

❏ We have examined how many church members are actually familiar with the church mission statement.

How?

❏ We have examined all structures of the church in view of their potential for multiplication.

With what result?

❏ All the leaders of the church have an apprentice leader (co-leader).

Names?

❏ All the leaders receive regular care and help from a supervisor/coach.

Names?

❏ For each of the different areas of ministry in the church, we have a responsible department leader.

Names?

❏ We have helped all church members to discover their spiritual gifts.

How?

❏ We have trained gift counselors.

How?

❏ The spiritual meaning of structural questions is communicated regularly in our church.

In what ways?

❏ We have developed a plan for church development.

What does it look like?

❏ The workers in our church are regularly trained.

Examples?

❏ The training program deals with contents that have been derived from the actual needs of workers.

Which needs?

❏ We have developed an organizational chart that reveals clearly the structure and areas of responsibility within the church.

What does it look like?

❏ We have presented the organizational chart to the church.

How?

❏ We have discovered ways to use the existing strengths of our church to improve the quality factor, "functional structures."

Which strengths?

❏ We have identified some barriers that seem to block the successful implementation of needed practical steps and we have met them in appropriate ways.

Examples?

❏ The results of our measures for improvement are monitored regularly.

When was this done last?

❏ The steps we are taking are evaluated according to biotic principles.

With what results?

❏ We have set a date for a new church profile.

When?

Other:

Part 3:
Quality
Characteristics

Quality Characteristic 5:
Inspiring Worship Service

"Nobody else but the Holy Spirit shall be the one who 'inspires' people."

The biblical motto selected for this quality characteristic reveals clearly what this quality characteristic is all about: The Holy Spirit (Latin: *spiritus*) is the one who "inspires"

Test Question: Is visiting the worship service an inspiring experience for church members? See NCD, pages 30-31

people. Our working view of worship services should aim at not "putting out the Spirit's fire." All the parts of a church service, from the seating arrangements to the music and to the message, should become more and more the vehicles through which the Spirit of God and God's love can be experienced in the community of Christians.

Biblical Motto: *"Be joyful always; pray continually; give thanks in all circumstances, for this is God's will for you in Christ Jesus. Do not put out the Spirit's fire."*

1 Thessalonians 5:16-19

When this quality characteristic appears as the current minimum factor of your church, it can have different causes, depending on the character of the church and the dominant theological paradigm. Thus the steps you will take will vary accordingly. It is obvious that the worship service is at the moment not yet the kind of church meeting it could be according to God's will. Evaluate any steps you take in this area by asking yourself: How can our worship services come to be described by participants as "inspiring"?

 Your Thoughts:

Please note here which of the following suggestions you feel have the greatest relevance for the situation of your church:

Practical Steps

Develop a worship preparation team.

The worship service should be led by a team where each member participates according to his or her gifts. A gift-oriented and inspired team is the cornerstone of an inspiring worship service. If such a team does not yet exist, it should be developed as quickly as possible. If it already exists, the following suggestions should be thought through carefully in this circle.

"A gift-oriented and inspired team of workers is the cornerstone of an inspiring worship service."

• *The following persons would be possible candidates for a worship preparation team:*

_____

_____

_____

Visit together the inspiring worship services of other churches.

Visit Other Churches

The meaning of "inspiration" can be described only imperfectly with words. It must be experienced. Find out where the truly inspiring worship services are celebrated in your vicinity. Visit these services with your worship preparation team. Don't fall into the trap of copying such services. The goal is to be sensitized for the dynamics of an inspiring worship service. For this reason, it is better to visit as many diverse worship experiences as possible. Also try to plan an interview with the local pastor or leader responsible for worship.

On _____ (date) I and our local worship team will visit the church service of the following out-of-town church:

_____

_____

_____

Evaluate how the messages could communicate more enthusiasm.

Evaluate Your Sermons

Preaching styles vary for different pastors. And that is good. It would be extremely counterproductive to try to imitate the preaching style of someone else. Sermons need to be "real." A pastor should not become a different person just because he preaches. His gestures, mimic, and choice of words should reflect his usual personality. There are, however, several points that a pastor should think through no matter what his preaching style is like:

1. Focus more strongly on *real questions* and needs of the listeners. Many pastors succumb to the illusion that their own questions are also the most urgent questions for their audience. Sermons should offer practical help based on the word of God.

2. You probably are used to outlining at least the main thesis of your sermons. In addition, you should develop the good habit before every sermon of writing down exactly the kinds of *changes* in the life of your congregation you hope to see as a result of your sermon.

3. Concentrate on subjects for which the church can also offer help in implementation. For instance, it makes sense to preach about our responsibility in certain social questions, if the church also offers a concrete project, and clarifies ways a person can get involved. If you call upon Christians to grow in love, make sure you first have organized cell groups where this kind of life can be practiced.

4. Illustrate the main points of your sermons with examples taken from the life of the local church. Why not speak about the couple who recently came to faith? Or, how about that small group that found a way to deal with a long standing conflict? Of course, we should be sensitive to distinguish which examples can be mentioned with the names of people and which need to be referred to anonymously, and which stories should never be told from the pulpit in the first place.

• *Use the following checklist before each of your sermons, and also when evaluating the worship service with your worship preparation team. What went especially well? In what areas do we have to make sure we improve our performance before next Sunday?*

Worksheet: Sermon Checklist

1. What urgent needs of those attending this service will this sermon address?

_____

_____

_____

_____

_____

2. What concrete changes will result in the life of the church members from this sermon?

_____

_____

_____

_____

_____

3. Which resources and opportunities in our church support the application of this sermon?

_____

_____

_____

_____

_____

4. Which examples from the life of our church can illustrate the main points of this sermon?

_____

_____

_____

_____

_____

Evaluate the Music

Evaluate your music and find ways to make it more inspirational.

There is hardly any other factor that contributes more to an inspiring spiritual worship atmosphere than music. This is also the area where you will find the most diversity in style (and "liturgical rules"), so that it is impossible to give you a single model useful for every church. In general, however, you should make sure that the music has a positive, enthusiastic quality. Almost every spiritual awakening has produced new songs. Being open to new, contemporary songs is therefore one of the numerous indicators for a church in renewal.

• *The following parts of our worship service are already quite inspiring in regard to the music:*

_____

_____

_____

_____

• *The following parts should be improved:*

_____

_____

_____

_____

• *The following steps need to be taken to make the suggested improvements a reality:*

_____

_____

_____

_____

Actively involve the greatest possible number of people in the church service.

Developing a Ministry Team

Two or three trained "lay liturgists," a greeting team welcoming first-time visitors and taking them to the sanctuary, Bible readings by catechists, songs presented by the children's Sunday School class, announcements by the church elder, a musical solo offered by a talented church member, testimonials by Christians reporting experiences with God—all these are possibilities of how to actively involve Christians with different gifts in a church service. The point is not to give as many people as possible a platform to promote "themselves", but rather to create a worship service that will be experienced by those who attend as attractive. Therefore, the quality of each contribution is important.

• *In addition to our current tradition we could involve church members in the following areas:*

_____

_____

_____

_____

• *To ensure that the contributions by church members will be of a high quality we will take the following steps:*

_____

_____

_____

_____

Welcoming First-time Visitors

Make sure not to overlook first-time visitors.

Churches have developed diverse systems to make first-time visitors—or persons who attend church only infrequently—feel as comfortable as possible. It is imperative for church members to welcome newcomers in a friendly way. Informal meetings—before or after the church service offering refreshments can be a big help in this area.

In some churches it works well to greet and meet first-time visitors right at the door. Other churches prefer to greet visitors during the church service, to identify them in order to present them with a small "welcome gift." Other churches have commissioned trained volunteers to meet visitors and introduce themselves.

• *How does your church identify first-time visitors?*

_____

_____

_____

_____

• *In addition to what is already happening, what could be done to make visitors feel comfortable and reinforce their desire to come again?*

_____

_____

_____

_____

_____

_____

Conduct a feedback session after each church service.

Make it your firm habit to not only plan future church services with your worship preparation team, but to also evaluate the most recent worship service. Critically review each part of the service (music, sermon, welcome, etc.) and ask yourself, "What could we do better next time?" Writing down all suggestions for improvement helps you keep track of how they are implemented. Also, from time to time it is profitable for these feedback sessions to include people that do not belong to the team, but who are part of the ministry focus group you are trying to reach. If your church service is focusing primarily on the unchurched, you should actually plan feedback sessions with them. If you have targeted families with small children, make sure they are included in your feedback group. It might be helpful to compile all the goals you are pursuing in your worship preparation on a special checklist which you can use to evaluate your services regularly. You might want to include some of the ideas from this chapter as building blocks for your list.

• *Appoint a person in your worship preparation team who will be responsible for leading the regular feedback sessions. You may want to also delegate the task of preparing an appropriate checklist. Who would be the right kind of person for this ministry?*

Monitor how effective your steps actually are.

In order to monitor your steps toward improving this factor, conduct another church profile after about six months. In this way you can examine if you need to continue your efforts in the area of this quality factor, "inspiring worship" or if you should move on to the next quality characteristic (your new minimum factor).

We will do a new church profile to monitor our progress on _____ *(date).*

Checklist: Inspiring Worship Service

❏ We have examined how well our worship style fits our church model, the number of visitors we have, the style of spirituality, and our ministry focus group. We have initiated changes where necessary.

Which changes?

❏ We have identified those members who have gifts that could be used for preparing our worship services.

Names?

❏ We have developed a plan to regularly involve more volunteers in the worship service.

What does the plan look like?

❏ We have built up a worship team that regularly develops and evaluates our worship services.

Who belongs to it?

❏ We offer training to all regular worship team members (public readings, music, sermons, worship leadership, etc.)

Who is leading this training?

❏ We have Christians with the gift of prayer who pray specifically for our church services. They receive appropriate information from our worship team.

When and where does this prayer take place?

❏ Each part of the service has been evaluated (songs, sermon, seating order, announcements, etc.) to see if they are designed creatively and spread a positive atmosphere.

The results of this evaluation?

❏ The sermons are regularly evaluated using the sermon checklist.

When was the last time?

❏ We have a designated time during the worship service for personal testimonies that illustrate how the Christian faith transforms everyday life.

What was the content of the last testimony?

❏ Each church service is evaluated critically by the worship team on the basis of a special checklist we developed, and each week we have suggestions for improvements.

What kind of checklist?

❏ During the church service, we offer a high quality children's program.

The names of the leaders?

❏ The children's ministry leaders are being trained and receive support from the church leadership.

What kind of training?

❏ We have developed several opportunities for social interaction before and after the church service.

What kind?

❏ We have designated members who spot first-time visitors in each church service and greet them.

Who?

❏ We have checked the time of the worship service to make sure it fits the needs of the majority of the visitors.

Result?

❏ We have found out how existing strengths in our church could be used to develop our church services.

Which strengths?

❏ We have identified obstacles to the implementation of the practical steps and have met them in appropriate ways.

Examples?

❏ The results of our measures for improvement are monitored regularly.

When was this done last?

❏ The steps we are taking are evaluated according to biotic principles.

With what results?

❏ We have set a date for a new church profile.

When?

Other:

Part 3:
Quality
Characteristics

Quality Characteristic 6: Holistic Small Groups

"Sometimes small groups are considered a subculture of the church, tolerated but suspect."

Some churches identify the quality characteristic "holistic small groups" as their minimum factor because they have practically no small groups to offer; other churches, because their small groups are not really focused on meeting the real questions and needs of their members in a holistic way. In other cases, there are a few groups which are holistically oriented but they do not aim at multiplying and including more and more people in their fellowship. Sometimes small groups are simply tolerated as a peculiar subculture that is a bit suspect, but not as a goal meant to be pursued with all creative means possible.

> *Test Question: Are the small groups dedicated to answering the true questions and meeting the real needs of its members in a holistic way?*
>
> See NCD, pages 32-33

The starting point in your church will naturally determine the practical steps you should take to improve the quality of this area. Simply imitating the successful models of other churches will work in only the rarest cases. For this reason, we have limited this chapter to the discussion of only such elements that demonstrably reflect principles of growing churches around the globe.

Biblical Motto:
"They broke bread in their homes and ate together with glad and sincere hearts, praising God and enjoying the favor of all the people."

Acts 2:46-47

Your Thoughts:

Please indicate here which of the following practical ideas are most relevant for the situation of your church:

Practical Steps

Make sure small group leaders are trained for their work.

The quality of a small group is literally dependent on the qualification of its leader. That's why it is so important that (a) only those persons who are spiritually gifted for this task be called as small group leaders, and (b) these Christians be well trained for their ministry.

"The quality of the small group depends literally on the qualification of its leader."

a. The most important gift that a small group leader should bring to this ministry is the gift of pastoring. This gift enables people to shoulder the long-term responsibility for the spiritual and personal welfare of a group of people. Our research indicates that this is one of the most widespread spiritual gifts, but it is often not exercised because of the misconception that pastoral ministry belongs to the classical tasks of a pastor. This is a big mistake. While the pastor does not necessarily need the gift of pastoring to be effective, a small group leader depends on it urgently. If you start the process of discovering spiritual gifts (see pages 56-58), you will notice that you have many more people with this gift in your church than you ever thought possible.

b. The gift of pastoring does not make good training for this ministry unnecessary. Each church should have a well organized system to prepare potential cell group leaders for their work. Some subjects might be: How do I lead a group discussion? How do I prepare a Bible study? How do I work for the multiplication of the group? How do I train an apprentice? Many churches offer this training themselves, others send their leaders to outside seminars.

- *The following Christians in our church have the gift of pastoring:*

_____

_____

_____

_____

_____

_____

_____

• *Our church offers the following training for (future) cell group leaders:*

_____

_____

_____

_____

_____

Training Apprentice Leaders

Pay attention to the consistent application of the apprentice leader principle.

The best method for continually raising up leaders for future groups is to first appoint possible candidates as apprentice leaders. Apprentice leaders can be introduced step by step to the task of planning and leading a group. During this process, it will be become obvious if God has equipped this person with the necessary gifts. One of the most urgent tasks of an existing leader is to spot and select apprentice leaders who can be trained on the job until they can lead a group all by themselves.

• *The following persons could be possible apprentice leaders for (current or future) cell groups:*

_____

_____

_____

_____

_____

Encourage Multiplication

Encourage a planned process of multiplication.

If the majority of Christians in a church were integrated in small groups of about six members, if each of these groups would win just one new person to Christ each year, the size of the church would double in this way within five years! It is a realistic goal for a small group to win one new person to Christ every year. But groups should not grow indefinitely. It is best to consciously set a size limit to your groups. Eight to ten group members is an optimal size. What should you do if this size is reached or even exceeded? Unfortunately, most churches do nothing—and soon realize that growth has stopped all by itself. Other churches decide at this point to divide the groups, which often leads to painful experiences. The best way to reach a continuous multiplication of groups is to find within the groups those members who can start a new group as "pioneers." This is much less painful than dividing the group into two halves. Each group should be committed to multiply. And, if possible, this multiplication should take place within the first year.

- In our church we can encourage the process of multiplication in the following ways:

_____

_____

_____

_____

_____

Have the courage to let some groups die.

Let Some Groups Die

If you speak about reproduction and multiplication, you must also speak about dying. This is the endpoint of a very normal growth process. Many groups, especially those who have existed for years, have long outlived their capacity to receive new members. But sometimes no one is courageous enough to end the group. A lot of energy gets expended that could be used in a more productive way. To dissolve a group can even be an occasion for celebration if it has birthed two daughter groups, six "grand children," and fifteen "great grand children." This is God's plan to multiply life.

- *The following groups in our church should be terminated:*

_____

_____

_____

_____

- *The members of these groups could profit more personally from the following programs and resources and contribute to the growth of the church:*

_____

_____

_____

_____

Use Appropriate Resources

Provide appropriate resources for the content development of the groups.

Group leaders do not have to come up with all the ideas for their group meetings themselves. Even the pastor does not have to be the "solo idea generator" for all groups. Thousands of groups have already positively experienced thousands of ideas. Why not profit from some of their ideas? What is important here is to evaluate all possible group resources to make sure they will have a positive impact on the growth of the church. Our institute is committed to creating group resources for each of the eight quality characteristics of natural church development. These resources link biblical impulses with practical exercises and methods from which a group can choose whatever fits their situation best.

• *In the future we will support our group leaders with the following resources:*

_____

_____

_____

_____

_____

_____

_____

_____

_____

Create Different Types of Groups

Make sure you have different types of groups.

One of the weaknesses of many churches is their insistence on one single type of groups. They value the fact that all their groups follow the same outline. But people and their needs vary, and this fact should be reflected in the way we design our group ministries. The more varied the choices, the more types of people you will be able to reach through your group ministries. Think about the possibilities of reaching different kinds of people through different types of groups.

• *The following types of groups that at present do not exist could fill the needs of members and/or non-members:*

_____

_____

_____

_____

• *The following persons would be able to lead these future groups:*

_____

_____

_____

_____

_____

Make the coaching of your group leaders your priority.

Caring for Groups Leaders

The training of small group leaders is an ongoing process. A well functioning system of groups depends on the constant guidance and resourcing of group leaders and the coordination of the work of the groups. In smaller churches, this central task can be done by the pastor. In larger churches it is important to develop two or more group coordinators who will devote their energies to this task.

• *In our church we continually resource and guide our group leaders in the following way:*

_____

_____

_____

_____

_____

• *We could improve this area in the following ways:*

_____

_____

_____

_____

_____

Monitor Your Progress

Monitor the effectiveness of your actions.

In order to monitor how effective your steps to improve this factor have been, you should conduct a new church profile after about six months. In this way you can examine if you need to continue your efforts in the area of this quality factor, "holistic small groups", or if your efforts have been so successful that you should move on to the next quality characteristic (your new minimum factor).

- *We will do a new church profile to monitor our progress on* _____ *(date).*

Checklist: Holistic Small Groups

❏ In our church the significance of small groups is regularly preached about.

When was the last time?

❏ The small group leaders receive appropriate training.

What kind of training?

❏ At least once a month there is a meeting for all group leaders for training and exchange of experiences.

Who leads out?

❏ Each group leader has recruited an apprentice.

Names?

❏ Group leaders are taught how to lead their groups towards multiplication.

In what ways?

❏ Group leaders have a supervisor/coach who meets with them at least once a quarter to evaluate the ministry and plan next steps.

Names?

❏ Today there are more groups than six months ago.

Which groups?

❏ The group leaders are regularly informed about growth and leadership resources.

Examples?

❏ We have checked that each group leader has the right gifts for his or her ministry.

How?

❏ The church leaders have an overall view of the size of all the groups: groups with 12 or more participants are prepared for multiplication.

When did it happen last?

❏ In several groups we have already identified "pioneers" who will be involved in starting new small groups.

Names?

❏ Small group leaders are supported purposefully by the church leadership.

How?

❏ We have investigated the needs of non-members which are not yet met by existing groups.

Examples?

❏ We have created groups that will try to meet these needs specifically.

Examples?

❏ We have found ways to apply the existing strengths of our church to develop the small groups.

Which strengths?

❏ We have identified some barriers that seem to block the successful implementation of needed practical steps and we have met them in appropriate ways.

Examples?

❏ The results of our measures for improvement are monitored regularly.

When was this done last?

❏ The steps we are taking are evaluated according to biotic principles.

With what results?

❏ We have set a date for a new church profile.

When?

Other:

Quality Characteristic 7: Need-oriented Evangelism

Part 3:
Quality
Characteristics

Test Question: Are the forms and contents of the evangelistic activities related to the needs of those you are trying to win? See NCD, pages 34-35

Many churches that do not experience growth logically conclude that "evangelism" has to be their minimum factor. They do not see that their growth can be hindered by deficits in very different quality characteristics. On the other hand, there are churches that have grown rapidly during the last few years, but their church profile indicates need-oriented evangelism as their minimum factor. These churches have a hard time identifying with their church profile. How else could you possibly explain their growth if not by successful evangelism?

What both churches do not recognize is that in view of quantitative growth, "evangelism" is but one of eight necessary building blocks.

To have "need-oriented evangelism" as your minimum factor may mean that there are simply too few evangelistic activities going on in your church. Another reason may be that the current evangelistic activities are not "need-oriented" enough. Whatever your starting position, the following suggestions will help you to noticeably improve the quality of ministry in this area. All these ideas are based on the assumption that evangelism is not just an isolated activity in the church, but part of the total long-term development of the church.

"All these ideas about evangelism have one common denominator—they place evangelism into the context of long-term church development."

Biblical Motto: *"To the Jews I became like a Jew... To those not having the law I became like one without the law. . . I have become all things to all men so that by all possible means I might save some."* 1 Corinthians 9:20-22

 Your Thoughts:

Please indicate here which of the following practical ideas are most relevant for the situation of your church:

Practical Steps

"Make sure that Christians with the gift of evangelism are relieved of other tasks if necessary."

Find out who in your church has the gift of evangelism.

It is important for the evangelistic program of your church to distinguish carefully between those who have the gift of evangelism and those who don't. In our work with the spiritual gift test we found confirmation for the thesis that God has given the gift of evangelism to about 10 percent of Christians. It is important for church leaders to know these persons. If your church has embarked on this process of gift discovery (more about this process on pages 56-58) you will know relatively soon who the 10 percent with the gift of evangelism are in your church. Make sure to relieve these people, if necessary, of other obligations in the church, to allow them to concentrate their full energy on evangelism. Help them to get intentionally and continuously involved in evangelistic ministry.

• *Who has the gift of evangelism in our church?*

_____

_____

_____

_____

_____

_____

_____

• *Besides these persons who are already involved in a direct evangelistic ministry, who is not yet involved who is gifted in evangelism?*

_____

_____

_____

_____

_____

_____

• *What can you do to help Christians with the gift of evangelism find enough time to be consistently involved in evangelistic ministry?*

_____

_____

_____

_____

_____

_____

_____

Relate all spiritual gifts more intentionally to the area of evangelism.

Involving All Spiritual Gifts in Evangelism

All spiritual gifts, not just evangelism, can be utilized in the evangelistic ministries of the church. It is important to help Christians to more strongly correlate their gifts to this minimum factor—namely "need-oriented evangelism." In most churches, gifts are used too much in the internal affairs of the church, which means that people who have no contact with the church are hardly touched by their ministry.

• *We want to help every Christian to use his or her gifts in such a way that people get to know Christ through their ministry:*

_____

_____

_____

_____

_____

_____

_____

Offer Gift-oriented Training for Evangelism

Conduct "The Three Colors of Evangelism" seminar in as many groups in the church as possible.

To support churches in their efforts to use a form of evangelism based on the different giftedness of Christians, our institute has developed the course "The Three Colors of Evangelism." (English edition not yet available. Please call for other suggestions.) This course can be used by individual Christians, but it is most helpful for small groups. In this basic course, the principles of natural church development are consistently applied to the factor "evangelism." We recommend this course, especially for those churches who have identified "need-oriented evangelism" as their minimum factor. If you use other resources, make sure not to expect the same from Christians who do not have the gift of evangelism that you would expect from Christians to whom God has given this gift. In their well meant intention to motivate people to participate in the fulfillment of the Great Commission, many resources for evangelism go simply too far. In addition, avoid any methods that champion manipulative or pushy evangelism tactics.

• *The following groups in our church are good candidates for a basic training course in principles of evangelism:*

_____

_____

_____

_____

_____

• *How could these groups be won for this concern?*

_____

_____

_____

Identify "Extended Families"

Help Christians to discover their "extended families".

The following ideas are meant for those 90 percent of church members to whom God has not given the gift of evangelism—because it is precisely their ministry that can contribute so much in the fulfillment of the Great Commission. The "extended family" are all those persons in the relational network of a Christian who do not have a personal relationship with Jesus Christ and His church (friends, relatives, colleagues). Please copy Worksheet 1 (appendix page 218) for each active Christian in your church. Make sure that each active member will receive a copy of this worksheet. You might even conduct a special evening or weekend seminar on "personal evangelism." If you already have a well organized system of small groups you may be able to fill out and discuss these worksheets in the context of your small groups. On the worksheet, people should fill in the names of those who belong to their "extended family." In a second step they are asked to underline the names of two persons they will focus on more fully in the future. They also commit themselves to daily pray for these persons, and work towards deepening their relationship with them.

• *On* _____ *(date) we will have a meeting to encourage each active member to identify his or her "extended family."*

Create Consciousness for a Potential Congregation

During the church service regularly make people conscious of the "potential congregation."

The "potential congregation" consists of the sum of all the people in the extended families of each active Christian. At this stage it is important to help your active church members keep this group of people in mind and recognize that they have responsibility for them. You can advance this process by asking for the filled out worksheets and putting them into an oversized envelope. Solemnly seal this envelope and hang it up in your worship room. Each time you assemble for worship, pray for the people whose names are contained in the envelope.

• *In each worship service we will pray for the "members of our potential church" starting on* _____ *(date).*

• *To encourage people to keep the "potential church" and its needs in their thinking, prayers and planning, we will do the following:*

_____

_____

_____

Establish Habitual Processes

In each group meeting reserve 10-15 minutes to talk about the "extended families."

To integrate the process of personal evangelism firmly in the life of the church it is important to refer to it at different occasions. After the members have identified their "extended families," make sure there is a regular time at the beginning or at the end of any group meeting to share experiences about this subject. It makes no difference if it is a small group, a choir or a church board meeting. During this time of interaction ask: "What progress have you made in your relationship with your "extended family"? Where do you have difficulties? What prayer requests would you like to make known? What could the church offer to assist your efforts?" Such interchange keeps the attention of the church focused and signals to every member that they are not alone in their endeavors.

• *In the following groups, it might be very possible to integrate inter-action about their "extended families" into the regular group program:*

_____

_____

_____

_____

_____

_____

Develop Need-oriented Opportunities

Create opportunities that zoom in on the needs of your "potential congregation."

If you concentrate your work on your "potential congregation", you are not dealing with an anonymous target group, but with people whose needs and problems you already know quite a bit about. No complicated surveys are necessary since you already have the best link to them imaginable—loving relationships with active church members. Make sure you learn from your church members where the members of their "extended families" have the greatest needs. This will give you a good indication where the church should put the emphasis in its program planning. Are relationship problems dominant? Economic problems? Drugs? Loneliness? Stress? Overweight? Difficulties in raising children? All these could be good subjects for church programs to which you could invite unchurched friends, relatives and colleagues.

• *After the Christians have talked with the members of their extended families, find out what needs they have identified. In a second step, brainstorm with them how the church might respond to each of these needs.*

_____

_____

_____

_____

_____

_____

Conduct special evangelistic events.

The above emphasis on the importance of personal relationships of church members to non-Christians does not mean that your church should limit itself to personal evangelism. On the contrary, in order to support individual efforts, specific evangelistic events are of great significance. While certain "classic" forms of evangelism are problematic, if viewed as isolated events, they are decidedly meaningful within the overall processes described in this book. The more evangelism has become part of the "lifestyle" of a church, the more each evangelistic activity will bear actual fruit.

• *During the next nine months, we are planning the following evangelistic events and activities to which church members can invite their friends, relatives and colleagues:*

Event or activity	Date

Help Assimilate New Christians

Help newly won Christians to be integrated into the church.

As long as new Christians have not become active members of the church, evangelism has stopped halfway. Most churches grossly underestimate how difficult it is for newcomers to find their place in the church. Existing groups do not usually behave as if they automatically integrate new visitors. The result is a terribly high relapse rate among those who have just come to faith. Integrate new Christians into the life of the church in such a way that they develop a sense of belonging and begin to participate actively in the life of the church. Some churches have had good experiences with the following steps:

- Appoint one member in each group who is responsible for the assimilation of new Christians. This person makes sure that new members are introduced to other group members and that the group receives them openly and warmly.

- Analyze the results of past efforts to integrate new Christians. What happened to those who came to believe in Jesus during the last two years? Into which group were they integrated? Have they found new friends in the church? Do they have a task that matches their giftedness? How many are still active in the church, how many have turned their back on the church?

- Take a survey of those persons who once attended, but who no longer grace the doors of a church. What was the reason for their departure? The lessons we learn through such conversations are invaluable because they help us avoid similar mistakes in the future.

- *What does your church do to intentionally improve the assimilation process of new Christians? What should be corrected? How?*

_____

_____

_____

_____

_____

_____

Monitor the effectiveness of your actions.

Monitor Your Progress

In order to monitor how effective your steps to improve this factor have been you should conduct a new church profile after about six months. In this way you can examine if you need to continue to concentrate your efforts in the area of the quality factor, "need-oriented evangelism", or if your efforts have already been so successful that you should move on to the next quality characteristic (your new minimum factor).

- *We will do a new church profile to monitor our progress on* _____ *(date).*

Checklist: Need-oriented Evangelism

❑ Our church has a departmental leader for evangelism.

Name?

❑ At least 60 percent of our small groups have conducted gift-oriented training for evangelism.

Which course?

❑ At least 50 percent of the small groups in our church have integrated interchange about their extended families at least once a month.

How do you make sure this is taking place?

❑ At least once a year, our church organizes public evangelistic events.

Which events?

❑ We know who the ten percent are who have the gift of evangelism in our church.

Names?

❑ The "evangelists" in our church have found ministries where they can use their gifts.

Examples?

❑ We provide guidance for our "evangelists."

Who does that?

❑ Our "evangelists" are supported regularly by prayer partners.

By whom?

❑ We know the names of our "potential congregation."

List of names?

❑ The needs of the potential church have been identified.

Results?

❑ Our church has created event that are tailored to the needs of our potential congregation.

For instance?

❏ There are Christians in our church who constantly think of new and unusual forms of evangelism.

Examples?

❏ We have a plan to help integrate each new person who has come to faith in Christ.

What does it look like?

❏ At least 30 percent of all church groups have been organized less than 12 months ago.

Which groups?

❏ New converts receive guidance in finding an evangelistic ministry that fits their spiritual giftedness.

How is this accomplished?

❏ We have found ways to apply the existing strengths of our church to intensify the evangelistic outreach of our church.

Which strengths?

❏ We have identified some barriers that seem to block the successful implementation of needed practical steps and we have met them in appropriate ways.

Examples?

❏ The results of our measures for improvement in this area are monitored regularly.

When was this done last?

❏ The steps we are taking are evaluated according to biotic principles.

With what results?

❏ We have set a date for a new church profile.

When?

Other:

Quality Characteristic 8:
Loving Relationships

"This is the area where most churches extravagantly overestimate their strength."

According to our experiences, the quality characteristic, "loving relationships", is the area in which churches tend to extravagantly overestimate their actual quality. In many Christian churches, cliques have developed with definite relationships and rituals. Those who participate in cliques experience them as quite comfortable. Thus they fail to see how outsiders can have hard time finding access to their clique. These Christians consider themselves as "warmhearted" and "open" towards newcomers, but they communicate—mostly unconsciously—the message: "You don't belong here."

Test Question: Are the relationships of the members of this church characterized by a high degree of love and affection? See NCD, pages 36-37

The quality characteristic "loving relationships" is linked, stronger than other factors, to the personal life of individual church members. As a church leader you will only make progress as you succeed in including as many Christians as possible into the processes that will help you to grow together in the quality of love.

Biblical Motto: "A new command I give to you: Love one another. As I have loved you so you love one another. By this all men will know that you are my disciples, if you love one another."

John 13:34-35

Your Thoughts:

Please note here which of the following suggestions you feel have the greatest relevance for the situation of your church:

Practical Steps

Make the subject of love the priority subject of the next few months.

Decide to make the theme of "Growing in Love" the priority subject for the next six months. Some churches have had good experiences with setting aside a "Month of Love." Sermons, Bible studies, small group subjects, seminars, and guest speakers can be opportunities to treat this subject from different angles and to create an awareness in your church of just how central this theme is in the Word of God. Make every effort to provide support for your members in developing the art of growing in love. Avoid appeals to guilt. Instead, work with positive examples of how you and other Christians have managed to make progress in this area.

"Some churches have had good experiences with setting apart a 'Month of Love.'"

• *During the next few months the theme of "love" can become the central subject of our church in the following ways:*

_____

_____

_____

_____

_____

_____

_____

Include as many groups as possible in the process of learning to love.

Starting Group Processes

To help individual Christians, Christian groups and whole churches to grow in love we have developed resources with the title, "The Learning Love Process". (English edition projected to be available: Spring 2002.) This resource is designed for use in small groups. For this reason, we have published a leader's guide to help group leaders with practical tips for three, six or twelve group meetings focusing on the subject of "love." Even though the principles of natural church development are not mentioned openly, they are the foundation for every practical exercise of the course. If you succeed in involving the majority of the groups in your church in this process of focusing on improving love, you will find that love will not only be a subject discussed in committees but one that penetrates the life of the church.

• *The following groups in our church should focus on the process of learning to love during the next few months:*

_____

_____

_____

_____

_____

_____

_____

Create Practical Opportunities for Application

Provide opportunities to exercise love in practical ways.

The "Learning Love Process" is designed—not only as a subject for discussion, but as a set of exercises to help Christians to apply the love commandment. If you decide not to use this resource, make sure that the process does not stop at discussing "love." Learning processes are most effective when there is an opportunity to apply practically what has been understood cognitively.

• *In the next six months we will create the following possibilities for our members to grow in the art of love:*

_____

_____

_____

_____

_____

_____

_____

Encourage Story Telling

Let people regularly tell stories of their progress in the Learning Love Process during the worship service.

Give your church members who are working in their groups according to the "Learning Love Process" an opportunity to share their experiences during the worship service. These experiences illustrate the fact that growth in love is possible and can impact the church positively. Contact individual Christians to see if they would be willing to share their experiences during the worship service. Enlist your small group leaders as supporters who can encourage people to share their testimony. Make it clear that those examples that seem to be the least spectacular are also of special interest. They illustrate that love penetrates the normal small things of everyday life.

• *During the next few weeks the following Christians could report their experiences in the Learning Love Process during the worship service:*

_____

_____

_____

_____

_____

_____

Make sure that the love of the church is also shared with those who are not part of the church.

Take a Look Also at Unchurched People

The first goal of the "Learning Love Process" is to deepen the relationships of Christians to each other and improve their quality. This process is also a precondition for the evangelistic attractiveness of the local church. Do not stop here. Some circles spread fuzzy warmth towards the inside, but are unable to show this love in a practical way to those who are not part of the church. Be careful to apply all the principles learned during the "Learning Love Process" to non-Christians. This process may turn out to be one of your greatest measures of improving church growth, even though the subject of church development may not even be mentioned in the process.

• *We will work in the following ways to extend our efforts to grow in loving more and more towards those who are not part of our church:*

_____

_____

_____

_____

_____

_____

_____

Monitor Progress *Monitor how effective your steps actually are.*

In order to monitor how effective your steps to improve this factor have been, you should conduct a church profile after about six months. In this way you can examine if you should continue to concentrate your efforts in the area of the quality factor, "loving relationships", or if your efforts have already been so fruitful that you can move on to the next quality characteristic (your new minimum factor).

- *We will do a new church profile to monitor our progress on _____ (date).*

Checklist: Loving Relationships

❑ In our church, there are regular sermons focusing on the significance of love in the life of the church.

When was the last time?

❑ We give concrete guidance of how love can be learned in our church.

Examples?

❑ The church has been introduced to the "Learning Love Process."

How?

❑ At least 60 percent of our small groups have worked through the workbook "The Learning Love Process".

Which groups?

❑ We have appointed a department director for the area "loving relationships."

Name?

❑ We have created room during the worship service so that people can share how they have experienced love from others.

When was the last time?

❑ In our church we have created opportunities to deepen personal relationships.

How?

❑ We carefully watch not to overburden staff members and volunteers so that there is no more time to take care of relationships.

How?

❑ We have developed strategies to extend our expressions of practical love also to those who are not part of our church.

What kind of strategies?

❑ The leaders of our church are known to always praise others and encourage people.

Who?

❏ We encourage Christians consciously to also get involved outside of the church context.

In what ways?

❏ We are training those who work in the church to handle conflicts constructively.

How?

❏ We have found out how the existing strengths in our church could be used to develop loving relationships.

Which strengths?

❏ We have identified obstacles to the implementation of the practical steps and have met them in appropriate ways.

Examples?

❏ The results of our measures for improvement are monitored regularly.

When was this done last?

❏ The steps we are taking are evaluated according to biotic principles.

With what results?

❏ We have set a date for a new church profile.

When?

Other:

Learning to Think "Biotically"

Natural church development aims at releasing those growth dynamics which God himself uses to build his church. But if this statement is to be more than just theological rhetoric, we have to ask: How does this happen practically? At this point we turn to the "six biotic principles" described in the book Natural Church Development (pages 61-82). This training program will help responsible leaders increasingly integrate the categories of biotic principles into their thinking and into their decisions—thus becoming more sensitive to God's growth "automatisms."

The Structure of the Training Program

"We should try to master this technique as perfectly as possible—in order to put it aside again."

Sometimes it seems that leaders of growing churches have developed a "sixth sense." When confronted with the same challenges and problems as other leaders, their efforts are usually crowned with some results that have a positive effect on the development of their church. What are they doing differently than others? It is a sense, often intuitive, for what we have called "God's growth automatisms." It is the conscious (or often, unconscious) application of "the biotic principles."

This kind of decision making is an art. But any art builds on some kinds of techniques. In order to learn a new art, we first master the appropriate techniques, so we can forget about them again. This training program will help you do this.

What Is the Practical Meaning of the Principles?

Any "biotic" decision is based on some six principles:

Principle 1: Interdependence

Principle 2: Multiplication

Principle 3: Energy transformation

Principle 4: Multi-usage

Principle 5: Symbiosis

Principle 6: Functionality

All biotic principles aim at setting free those spiritual growth automatisms God uses to build His church.

See NCD, pages 12-14

These six principles are not in competition with one another, they are different answers to the same line of questioning: "How can we create conditions that will allow the potential that God has put into the church to unfold?" This training program will help to turn these concepts, which at first seem a bit abstract, into something fruitful for the decision-making processes of the church.

How You Can Proceed

For each principle, we suggest several exercises which will help you train yourself in biotic decision making. Please note that none of the chapters is intended to work through the complete solution of the case study. Only those aspects linked to the principle under discussion are to be practiced. A complete solution for the case studies discussed in the chapters will be found only in Training Unit 7.

Suggestions for Learning Together

At the end of each training unit you will find a section called "suggestions for learning together." In this section you will receive pointers for group learning sessions (e.g.: church board, church leadership team, small group leaders), including how to assess situations using the perspectives of natural church development and make biotic decisions.

In this section you will find no instructions to structure the exercises (how to combine different exercises, how often to meet to practice biotic thinking). This will vary from situation to situation. One possibility is to conduct an intensive training course over several weeks—starting with an informative evening followed by weekly evening programs devoted to deepening one biotic principle after another. Or try a short practical introduction to biotic principles during a Saturday seminar or an evening program. Select the right exercises from the following pages or develop your own! If you decide to do the training as a group, it is advantageous if all group members also work through the program individually.

It is neither necessary nor recommended that the whole church go through this training program. The less the leadership responsibility of group participants, the more you should avoid all "biotic jargon." However, those Christians who have leadership responsibilities in a church are strongly encouraged to study these techniques at least once in their lives.

✏️➤ Your Thoughts:

I would like to work through the training program "Learning to think biotically" until _____ (date).

The "suggestions for group learning" could be worked through with the following groups:

_____

_____

_____

_____

_____

Training Unit 1: Interdependence

"Too often we find out that a successful short-term solution produces exactly the opposite long-term effects."

A few years ago, one of the southern Indian provinces was hit by a cobra plague. These not so harmless snakes had multiplied until suddenly you could find them everywhere—in the streets, in houses, on the fields, and in the stables. The state

Test question: Are the long-term effects that this step has on other areas of the church organism beneficial for the development of the church or not? See NCD, pages 66-67

authorities stepped in and promised a head fee for each dead cobra. At first, the situation changed according to expectations. The citizens organized "cobra hunts" and the number of cobras dropped markedly. There was even a new profession that developed—professional cobra hunters could be frequently seen.

Yet after the initial decline of the cobra population, the authorities were shocked to learn that cobras could again be found everywhere. After investigating this phenomenon they found that many snake hunters had become snake breeders, thus securing their head premiums. The same measure that was supposed to decimate the number of cobras had, in the long run, the opposite effect.

Recognizing Interdependent Links

Such "cobra effects" can be observed also in Christian churches. Frequently, measures which are successful in the short run produce exactly the opposite of the desired outcomes in the long run. For example, if you help Christians discover their spiritual gifts but fail to help them find suitable areas of ministry, you may see their initial excitement soon dwindle to frustration. Many may become "immunized" against the very concept of gift-oriented ministry.

The principle of interdependence helps us to recognize, (a) how the different areas of church development are interconnected and dependent on each other, and (b) how changes in one area might have long-term ramifications, positive or negative, for other areas.

Exercise 1: Think through the different areas of the work of the church and write down some of these areas that you see interconnected to other spheres of ministry. The first two lines of the following columns are merely an example of what your list could look like.

Interdependent Areas	Kind of Linkage
Children's service and worship service	Many parents are won through their children
Gifts and tasks	Tasks are better done if they correspond to spiritual gifts
_____	_____
_____	_____
_____	_____
_____	_____
_____	_____
_____	_____
_____	_____
_____	_____
_____	_____
_____	_____

Recognize the Opposite of Interdependence

Sometimes it is easier to develop a sense for the correct approach by first identifying some negative examples. Just think of the mentioned "cobra effect"! The opposite of interdependence is the isolated perspective. To view something from an isolated perspective will lead to short-term successes; interdependent thinking will result in long-term fruitfulness.

We are not against short-term successes, but they must not be counterproductive in the long run. Unfortunately they all too often are. The church might be really tempted to invite the star evangelist once a year to do its share of evangelistic involvement. There is great joy if unreached persons have been invited and some of them give their heart to Christ. "Fifteen converts at the annual evangelistic meetings," reports the church newsletter. The (short-term) success can be documented. We seldom investigate the long-term results of such an activity; and when it is investigated, we are often disenchanted. In many cases we do not succeed in assimilating new converts in the church. Some who made a decision for Christ without experiencing the life-changing consequences of this decision are now "immunized" against any future call for a decision. Many members working in the church are actually crippled in their own evangelistic engagement since they have "delegated" their evangelistic responsibility to the external evangelist. The professional approach and the charisma of the outside evangelist make it difficult for the ten percent in your church who have the gift of evangelism to actually discover this gift in themselves. And on it goes. We have to think through all consequences when we think about the so-called success of any measure.

To exercise biotic thinking, we need to train ourselves to collect different possibilities and to evaluate each of them according to biotic principles. It might be helpful to first look for possible negative points: How much is this step linked to values that contradict the principle of interdependence (or any other biotic principle)? Our goal is not to develop a generally negative attitude towards all new steps, rather to learn to critically self-evaluate our own ideas in light of biotic values.

Exercise 2: Try to collect some examples of such negative relationships in your own church life. When have you approached a goal from an isolated perspective? What were the short-term successes? Why is the long-term fruit more suspect? Note this example.

Isolated Measure	Short-term Success
Christians discovery seminar	Christians are excited about their new discoveries

Now that you are sensitized, you can begin to practice concrete examples of "interdependence." The purpose of the following exercise is not to come up with a comprehensive and perfect solution. We only want to sharpen and expand your view for interdependencies in your church. You should also become aware of connections that may not have anything to do with the later solution.

Developing Interdependent Measures

You will find the description of two situations (you can add a third example from your own church context). The first is a "typical" problem that concerns the whole church. Second, you'll find a more pastoral problem which, at first sight, has little to do with church growth, but in principle any church can get into a similar situation.

To help you explore interdependencies, we have listed open-ended questions to stimulate—not limit—your creativity. Write down your thoughts. After some practice in biotic thinking, you will notice that you are reaching out intuitively to new, creative solutions.

Exercise 3: Read the two examples and note your solutions to the following guiding questions below on Worksheet 2 (page 219.) Please copy the worksheet as needed. At the end of this exercise, you will find our thoughts about how to possibly approach problem 2 from the perspective of interdependence. Before you read our suggestions, make sure you have written down your own thoughts. Then do the same exercise with an actual problem from your church (it is best to choose a clearly defined situation).

Problem 1: The evangelistic involvement of the church members is very low. Only a few people are led to Christ. What could be done about it?

Problem 2: The marriage of a team member of the children's ministry is in crisis. The spouses have separated. How could you react?

Problem 3: Look at one of the most pressing problems in your own church:

_____

_____

_____

_____

_____

Guiding Questions

1. *Which areas of ministry are affected in the short and in the long run by this problem? For your reflection use Worksheet 2 (page 219), based on the eight quality characteristics. You might add some subcategories such as "children's service" under "worship service," or "gift counseling" in the "ministry" section of the worksheet.*

2. *What could be done in these eight areas (and other sub-areas), short-term and long-term, to improve the situation described in the examples? Note your responses on a new copy of the same worksheet.*

A Suggested Approach

On the following pages you will see our thoughts for Example 2 (the marriage of a team member of the children's service going through a severe crisis). Of course, this is not a model solution or the only right solution. And we don't want to give the impression that problems like this always need to be tackled with biotic checklists using special worksheets. Our completed worksheet only illustrates how problems we encounter can be approached from a perspective of interdependence. You'll be surprised at how differently this marriage problem of a leader presents itself when viewed from this perspective.

The next two pages contain answers to question 1 *(Which areas of ministry are affected?)* and question 2 *(What could be done in the different areas?).*

Reflect on Your Own Thoughts

After you have worked through the exercises, use Worksheet 3 (page 220) to think about how you went about finding your solutions. Reflection about your own thought processes is one of the best ways to practice new categories of thought. How did you find a solution to Exercise 3? What thought strategies did you use? How did you work over and improve your solution, maybe even after you read our suggested solution?

Exercise 4: Using Worksheet 3, take at least 15 minutes to reflect on your own thought process as you found solutions to Exercise 3.

Worksheet: Develop a Network of Steps

Problem: _The marriage of one of the children's service team members is in a crisis—which areas are affected?_

Area concerned:	short-term	long-term
Leadership	_Pastor_	_Pastor_
	Leader of the children's service	_Leader of pastoral counseling_
Ministry	_Can she continue?_	_Does the marriage suffer from_
	Gift counselor: alternatives?	_an overload of church work?_
Spirituality	_Prayer team: prayer request_	_General: How do we deal_
		with divorce?
Structures		_Are there weaknesses in_
		coaching our team members?
Worship service	_Who will prepare the children's_	_Do we have to find a_
	service for next week?	_permanent replacement?_
Small groups	_Call small group leader_	_How will the cell cope: is addi-_
		tional worker training necessary?
Evangelism		
Relationships	_Small group members_	_Children's church team_
		Other team members

Worksheet: Develop a Network of Steps

Problem: _What can be done to contribute to a solution?_

Area concerned:

	short-term	long-term
Leadership	_A meeting with the pastor_	_Relate empowerment to personal areas_
Ministry		_Find new team member_
Spirituality	_Prayer team intercedes for the marriage_	
Structures	_Improve mentoring/coaching of leaders and team members_	
Worship service	_Ask other Children's-Church team to take over_	
Small groups	_Small group focuses totally on helping the team member in trouble._	_Train small group leaders for similar situations._
Evangelism		
Relationships	_Encourage friends to practice genuine friendship_	

Suggestions for Learning Together

If you would like to use the exercises suggested in this chapter in a group setting such as your church leadership team, keep in mind the following guidelines:

1. Before you conduct the exercises, group members need a basic knowledge of interdependence. This can be acquired by the group members working through this book individually (in conjunction with *Natural Church Development*, which is recommended for persons with wider leadership responsibilities), or by your short introduction to the subject (recommended for a group of other team members in the church).

Create a Basic Understanding

2. "A picture says more than a thousand words." An abstract word like "biotic principle," can be easily illustrated and lead people to experience the "aha" effect." Find images, pictures, and stories when you explain the principle of interdependence to your group members. Open, for instance, with the story of the cobra plague (page 126). Avoid too many biotic terms. Your group should learn to think biotically, not speak biotically.

Use Illustrations

3. Always begin with an easy exercise. If you are pushed for time and you can't do all the exercises, don't start with a complex exercise like Exercise 3. This exercise already presupposes some knowledge about the principle of interdependence which was developed in the previous exercises.

From the Simple to the Complex

4. During each exercise, plan enough time for evaluation. The great advantage of group learning is the chance to reflect on experiences together.

Plan to Evaluate Regularly

If you conduct Exercise 1 in your group, start with the story of the cobra plague (or an alternative story, such as the one about the elephant reservation in *Natural Church Development*, page 64).

Instructions to Exercise 1

Continue with a brainstorming session. If your group is larger than five persons, it is helpful to form smaller groups. Let everyone call out areas of the church and its ministry where he or she sees some kind of linkage to other areas. At this stage it is not important to go into detailed explanations of interdependence. All items should be written down by one of the group members.

During the next phase, have the group bring up each of the suggested areas of interdependence and discuss the effects of the observed linkages between two areas. Usually participants bring up obvious relationships as well as more hidden evidences. They will observe trite as well as essential aspects of interdependence, and sometimes cite even strange or far-fetched examples. Such contributions do not have to be "straightened out" because the goal of the exercise is to get into the theme and increase our awareness of interdependent realities in the church.

Instructions to Exercise 2

As long as you are working on training biotic thinking, ask your group members to talk only about examples of their *own* work in the church: Where did you take an isolated step, only to discover that the success was only temporary? This approach will prevent people from focusing on those things they never liked about somebody else's ministry. And when we discover the questionable aspects of our own decisions, the learning impact is increased considerably.

Ask the participants to first do the exercise by themselves. Then divide the group into triads (subgroups of three) for sharing their examples. Then let each subgroup contribute their most important insights. List them on an overhead slide or on the flip chart as you discuss:

What are the effects of isolated measures?

What are some of the reasons for rating some short-term successes negatively from a long-term perspective?

What would have happened if the problem had been approached from an interdependent perspective?

Instructions to Exercise 3

Before you will work in your group on a real live problem in your own church, first work through at least one of the case studies in this chapter.

You will need two copies of Worksheet 2 (page 219) for each example for each participant (for three participants working on one example you would need a total of six copies).

Give a short introduction, along the thoughts contained in the section "Developing interdependent measures" (page 129).

Indicate the example you have selected and ask the group members to first work individually through the worksheet using Guiding Question 1.

After about 15 minutes, ask the participants to divide into triads and share their ideas.

Let each person individually work through the second Guiding Question using another copy of the same worksheet.

After about 20 minutes ask the participants to divide again into triads to share their ideas and develop a group version of their responses (time: 15 minutes).

In the final plenary session, these group solutions will be presented and listed on the flip chart while discussing the following questions:

What "aha" experiences did group members have?

How can the principle of interdependence be used effectively in the example discussed?

The moderator of this group process should mention that not all eight areas will be involved with every problem the church faces. Note that the factor "evangelism" was not touched in the example on pages 131 and 132.

If you are doing Exercise 3 with your group, don't miss Exercise 4 either. Every participant evaluates the group session (15 minutes). Follow up with a time of sharing in triads. Then each triad is asked to make a list of successful and unsuccessful thought strategies with which all participants can identify (even if they have not applied them themselves). Conclude with presenting these lists to the whole plenary group.

Instructions to Exercise 4

<table>
<tr><td>Part 4:
Learning to think
biotically</td><td></td></tr>
</table>

Training Unit 2: Multiplication

"The opposite of multiplication in church development is not division, but addition."

Imagine a water lily growing on a pond with a surface of 14,000 square feet. The leaf of this species of water lily has a surface of 15.5 square inches. At the beginning of the year the water lily has exactly one

Test question:Does this step contain multiplication dynamics or does it merely contribute to addition?

See NCD, pages 68-69

leaf. After one week there are two leaves. A week later, four. After sixteen weeks half of the water surface is covered with leaves. How long will it take until the second half of the pond will also be covered? Another sixteen weeks? No. It will take just a single week and the pond will be completely covered. Sure enough, in the 17th week the leaves would cover over 14,000 square feet. After week 17 there would be 131,072 leaves covering 14,108 square feet.

This example demonstrates the potential behind the biotic principle of multiplication, but it reveals that it is not always simple to understand this principle. Many people have difficulties with the water lily exercise. At first, it's difficult to grasp why it would take only one week to cover the second half of the pond, if the first half took an entire sixteen weeks. But that's how the principle of multiplication functions.

A Modest Wish

Maybe you are familiar with the story of the inventor of the chess game, who was given one free wish as his reward by a king in India. As a most "modest" reward he wished just for a bit of rice on the first square of the chess board, two kernels on the second square, four on the third, eight on the fourth, and so on. This wish simply could not be granted by the king, who had smiled at it initially. He would have had to produce 2^{63} kernels of rice which is 9,223,372,036,000,000,000 kernels, or 153 billion tons of rice—more than the world rice harvest for the next 1000 years!

A Small Cause— but a Big Effect

The principle of multiplication illustrates clearly that natural church development is not about using more energy for church growth. "Work smarter, not harder" is the motto. As you strive for multiplication at all levels in the church, you are releasing an energy potential that cannot be attained any other way.

This is why we find this principle in the Bible from the beginning. Jethro counseled his son-in-law, Moses, to not decide all the legal cases himself, but rather to appoint helpers responsible for 10, 50, 100 and 1000 Israelites (Exodus 18). Moses was to "multiply" himself. The form of discipleship practiced by Jesus is nothing less than the application of the principle of multiplication in the area of "leadership development." Behind the New Testament *oikos* principle

(Greek for "house," here referring to a person's network of family, friends, colleagues, etc.), which is always the key for effective evangelism, you will also find the principle of multiplication: Every person who comes to faith in Jesus lives in a network of relationships (*oikos*) to a group of non-Christians. When a church starts to use these existing "bridges," it initiates an enormous multiplication impulse: New Christians who come to Jesus and into the church bring with them their *oikos*, which need ministry by the church. A multiplication process without limits has started, even though the beginnings may have looked so insignificant.

The opposite of multiplication in the work of the church is not division, but rather a conceptual preoccupation with mere addition. Approaching ministry from an addition perspective is different from the principle of multiplication in three ways:

The Technocratic Trap: Addition

1. The growth potential of addition is smaller than that of multiplication.

Smaller Growth Potential

Research through our institute has found that churches which consciously value the multiplication of small groups through division will experience growth more frequently than churches who do not pay attention to it. The largest local church in the world in Seoul, Korea (currently 750,000 members), was able to grow to this size only because the principle of multiplication was carefully observed from the beginning. Whoever takes a closer look at this church will notice that it really consists of a network of sub-congregations that originated through multiplication. These sub-congregations are then built on a network of continuously multiplying small groups. (We should mention in parenthesis that, as a rule, small churches are usually the more effective multipliers. The larger a church, the more its potential for multiplication normally decreases.)

Exercise 5: Note some examples of addition in your own church. What effect would the conscious application of the principle of multiplication mean in these cases? How does the potential for growth differ in both approaches? The first line of the following table gives you an example of what the result of your reflection could look like.

Addition	Multiplication	Differences in growth potential
Evangelistic campaign	Evangelism through *oikos* relationships	*Oikos* evangelism has limitless potential for multiplication
_____	_____	_____
_____	_____	_____
_____	_____	_____
_____	_____	_____
_____	_____	_____
_____	_____	_____
_____	_____	_____

More Impressive Results

2. At first sight, the addition approach seems to work for a greater visible result.

Technocratic church growth approaches always build on growing to an unlimited size. The goal is a megachurch, not the small constantly multiplying church (in this case the mother church would have to give up some of its members!); the large evangelistic meeting, not the quiet but continuous kind of evangelism through oikos relationships; the "best" and biggest leadership college, not the tedious process of discipleship Jesus opted for.

Multiplication usually needs a longer introductory phase but leads to better results in the long run. Remember the rice on the chess board squares: The advocates of the addition strategy might have asked for a few hundred bags of rice on each square, which certainly would have impressed the king, but in the end they would have received substantially less than the inventor of chess.

Exercise 6: In the following table note again a few examples of addition (you are free to use examples from exercise 5). For each, indicate the possible short-term and long-term successes of the suggested measure. Try to also list some examples that are consciously using the principle of multiplication. The first line again contains an example.

Measures based on addition	Short-term result	Long-term result
Evangelistic campaign	Many decisions during the meeting	Weakening of the evangelistic potential of the members
_____	_____	_____
_____	_____	_____
_____	_____	_____
_____	_____	_____
_____	_____	_____
_____	_____	_____

Measures based on addition	Short-term result	Long-term result
Oikos evangelism	At first relatively few "evangelistic successes"	More integrated Christians who are again evangelistically active
_____	_____	_____
_____	_____	_____
_____	_____	_____
_____	_____	_____
_____	_____	_____
_____	_____	_____

3. Addition aims at higher "production," multiplication at higher "production capacity."

Neglect of the "Production Capacity"

This difference—possibly the most important one—between addition and multiplication has been described by the Greek poet, Aesop, in his famous fable: A man owned a goose which laid for him a golden egg every day. At first the man anxiously fed and cared for his goose in order not to lose his source for gold and money. But then his greed took over as he thought about how to get more gold out of the goose. So he decided to butcher the goose to get to all the golden eggs at once, and that was the end of the golden eggs.

Do you have an idea for a biotic solution for more golden eggs? We don't know if the golden eggs were capable of being hatched—but the most meaningful solution would have been to grow more geese capable of laying golden eggs. Thus there would have been first an increase in "production capacity" and then in actual "production."

Exercise 7: Evaluate how your solutions for multiplication in Exercises 5 and 6 aim at augmenting "production capacity." If not, revise your solutions accordingly.

Measures based on multiplication	Increasing production capacity
"Oikos" evangelism	New converts are encouraged to share the gospel in their circle of friends
_____	_____
_____	_____
_____	_____
_____	_____
_____	_____
_____	_____

What Do You Do If There Is Zero Growth?

This originally economic term, "zero growth," is a contradiction in itself: either something grows or it does not. It is better called stagnation. Since stagnant churches are so widespread, you might have thought as you were reading, "These ideas are great, but I would be satisfied to just see some addition!" But this attitude overlooks the fact that addition thinking is often one of the *causes* for stagnation.

Consider the small group which has survived the last few years with some ten to twelve participants. From time to time there is a newcomer, but someone else leaves. There is no apprentice leader, which makes it impossible to think in terms of division. And the very thought of dividing the group is frowned upon because this would destroy their "great fellowship." This kind of thinking is additive zero growth.

Think of that church that conducts an evangelistic week with an invited evangelist once a year. Even though the week tends to be an event for insiders, and only few come to belief in Christ, the church does not consider multiplication approaches to evangelism. When the evangelistic week is evaluated (which happens rarely enough), the best solution is usually to find a better evangelist the following year ("who will preach the gospel more clearly"), to start the public advertising campaign earlier, or to use more contemporary posters. This kind of thinking comes with additive zero growth.

Then, consider the pastor with the gift of counseling who understands his role as primarily that of a counselor. Day by day, members of the church come with their questions and problems. Since his time is limited (and since he has already reduced other areas of his work in the church) he starts a waiting list. Currently he manages up to five appointments a day. But the waiting list keeps growing. He is thankful that his ministry in the church is so well received. So he lengthens his workday. From his perspective, the church is growing (or at least his work is). This active pastor will continue to expand this work until he burns out. However, seen through the lens of natural church development, the pastoral ministry of the church has not really grown. Real growth would require that he invest himself in training and coaching more lay "pastors," but for that he simply has no time left. This kind of thinking is again additive zero growth.

Exercise 8: In the following table, jot down some examples of additive zero growth in your own church. Ask about the short-term and long-term consequences. Then think again about possible multiplication alternatives.

Addition based zero growth	Short-term result	Long-term result

Multiplication based growth	Short-term result	Long-term result

Concerns about a Slow Beginning

We have noted that addition strategies are initially more impressive, and multiplication strategies initially require more starting time. One of the reasons that churches tend towards addition steps is the desire to see quick results. Few people have a long perspective or show endurance. For this reason we are often scared of processes that take more time. We fear that after six months someone might say, "I told you right away that it would not work," while we would still need half a year to see the first small results. The consequence is a preference for actions that bring short-term success even if they turn out to be failures in the long run.

Exercise 9: Use the following list of key words to identify barriers towards multiplication thinking. How strongly do these issues apply to you? What could be done about them?

	Tends to apply to me	Tends to not apply to me
Lack of endurance and patience	❏	❏
Pressure to see quick results	❏	❏
Not content with small beginnings	❏	❏
Difficulties to motivate people for the long haul	❏	❏
Inner barriers against multiplication thinking	❏	❏

Developing Multiplication Measures

Now proceed to find multiplication solutions for both of our examples and your own in the last chapter. Just remember that the goal is not to find the complete solution, but just to develop sensitivity for solutions that are compatible with the principle of multiplication.

Exercise 10: Read again the two examples on page 129, and using a copy of Worksheet 4 jot down your answers to each of the guiding questions. You will need a copy for each of the examples. At the end of this exercise, you will find our own suggestion on how the problem in Example 2 could have been approached from a multiplication perspective. After this example please address the issue you selected concerning your own church.

Guiding Questions

1. *Which aspects of multiplication could contribute to a solution for this situation? Develop concrete suggestions under the heading "growth potential," "long-term effect," and "extending the production capacity."*

2. Evaluate your proposals carefully:

• *What would an addition solution look like? Has your solution a greater potential for growth?*

• *Is the long-term effectiveness of your solution greater (even if it takes longer in the beginning)?*

• *What, in this example, has to do with "production"? What is "the production capacity" here? Does this solution really increase the latter?*

This Is How You Could Have Proceeded

Here are our thoughts to Example 2. It is not a "model solution," but an example of one of the many possible solutions of how the principle of multiplication can be applied. As in the case of the principle of interdependence, you will notice how differently a situation appears when you approach it with the help of biotic principles. An individual case of pastoral care can become a trigger for more comprehensive church growth processes.

Which elements of multiplication could be contained in this situation?

In a solution characterized by addition, the minister would focus exclusively on the individual case and try to help the leader through counseling. The best result possible would be a marriage saved— adding (in the best of scenarios) a new success to other solved cases.

A solution that aims at multiplying capacity would also pay attention to the marriage—at first. Immediate pastoral help is necessary. But while the addition solution would stop here, the multiplication approach would search for ways to increase capacity. A "production" goal would be to have as many team members as possible have healthy marriages and being able to offer them effective help during times of crisis. "Production capacity" refers to the ability of the church to accompany workers holistically in their ministry and offer them counseling.

This could mean that departmental leaders and coaches need to be trained to guide workers before there are problems. These leaders would have apprentice leaders being trained in the job for this ministry so that the coaching structure could grow along with the ministry.

Something similar could also be done for the counseling ministry: Here counselors who are trained in marriage counseling could transfer their know-how to counseling trainees who are watching them in action.

Consider encouraging the worker now going through the crisis to share his learning experience (after successfully weathering his own marriage crisis) with other couples. This could be done in a small group for couples that meets for some predetermined period of time using appropriate marriage strengthening resources.

The long-term effect of this solution would be an improvement of the coaching ministry for those working in the church before there is a crisis, a broader foundation of the counseling ministry in the church, and last but not least, a person helped through counseling would learn how to help others.

This case study has been presented in idealistic terms. Most of the problem cases of this kind will not lead to such comprehensive processes in church development. The case study simply illustrates the meaning of multiplication based interventions—that it starts way before those high flying growth goals for the church are conceived.

Reflect on Your Thinking

Evaluate the preceding exercise by reflecting on your own thought process. Using Worksheet 3 ask, How did you find solutions to Exercise 10? What thought strategies did you use? How did you work over and improve your solution, maybe even after you read our suggested solution?

Exercise 11: Using Worksheet 3 (page 220) take at least 15 minutes to reflect on your own thought process as you found solutions to Exercise 10.

Suggestions for Group Learning

As you plan the following group exercises, remember the guidelines already mentioned in the preceding chapter:

1. Before you conduct the exercises, group members should have a basic knowledge of multiplication.

2. Use images, pictures, and stories when you explain the principle of multiplication to your group members and watch for those "aha" effects.

3. Always begin with an easy exercise.

4. During each exercise, plan enough time for evaluation.

Introduction

One way to introduce the principle of multiplication is to present the example of the water lily pad (page 136). Ask the group members to spontaneously estimate how long it will take the water lily to cover the second half of the pond. In your own words, explain the principle of multiplication and discuss with the group why some estimated wrongly. Or select an even more impressive introduction: Get two chess boards and two one-pound bags of rice. Divide the group into two subgroups, the addition group and the multiplication group. Ask the groups to divide the rice onto the squares of the chess board. The group that needs the least squares to place all rice kernels on the board wins. The addition group can place up to 100 kernels of rice on each square, while the multiplication group has to start with one kernel on the first square, two on the second, four on the third, eight on the fourth, and so on. (Both groups are allowed to put piles of rice for each square beside the actual chess board squares which will turn out to be too small. It is best to also provide a calculator.)

The spontaneous reaction of the multipliers is often: "We will never get this bag used up. This is unfair!" But after a short time, it becomes obvious that the addition group does not have enough squares to use up their rice, while the multiplication group runs out of rice in the third row—and wins.

Evaluation: Discuss the differences between addition and multiplication, paying attention to such questions as potential for growth and short-term and long-term effects.

Instructions to Exercise 5-8

Exercises 5-8 are best done individually by each group member. Discuss the results of each exercise in groups of three. Then collect all the examples in the plenary group and work through the three best ones, paying attention especially to the aspects of "growth potential," "long-term effect," and "increasing production capacity" (and in Exercise 8 to the difference between short-term and long-term results).

Instructions to Exercise 10

Exercise 10 summarizes the points of all the other exercises and is therefore more difficult.

Before you work through a "live" example from your own church, you should work through at least one of the examples in this book. Copy Worksheet 4 (page 221) for each participant for each example to be worked on.

Indicate which problem is to be worked on, then ask the participants to work through the questions of Worksheet 4 individually.

After twenty minutes, ask participants to share their thoughts in groups of three. After fifteen minutes, evaluate each group's solution.

In the plenary group, bring together the collected solutions, sorted into categories; "growth potential," "long-term results," and "increase in production capacity." The best way to do this is to draw three columns on an overhead slide or a flip chart and list all the suggested solutions. When you are finished, go through the list evaluating the ideas on the basis of the questions contained in the worksheet.

Instructions to Exercise 11

Every participant evaluates the group session (15 minutes). Follow up with a time of sharing in triads. Each triad is asked to make a list of successful and unsuccessful thought strategies with which all participants can identify (even if they have not applied them themselves). Conclude with presenting these lists to the whole plenary group.

Training Unit 3: Energy Transformation

Test question: Is this measure utilizing the energy relationships of the environment, or trying to fight them?

See NCD, pages 70-71

The best example of the opposite of this principle of energy transformation can be studied at boxing matches. Two massive bodies punching each other. The tactic of both fighters is always the same: first to ward off the punch of the opponent with all his energy, then to initiate his own offense and use all his force to knock out the opponent. We have allowed this boxer mentality to enter many areas of church life: using force to annihilate the opposing forces, then using force again to reach the intended goal.

"Many areas of the life of the church have been invaded by a boxer's mentality."

This is exactly the underlying pattern of the approach that claims that "all Christians are evangelists." Guilt is created through appeals in order to attain the goal of increased evangelistic activity. This tactic settles for nothing less than getting a decision from each member to participate regularly at evangelistic efforts. Those who are not gifted evangelistically resist this approach.

Examples of the Boxer Mindset in Our Churches

Another example would be the hiring of a new minister, then attempting to finance his position through more intense calls for contributions to the church budget. Leaders are astonished that it is so difficult to motivate members to increase their giving for the local church. Many don't realize that the resistance to give to an organization is usually greater than the willingness to give to a real person.

A cell group has reached the upper limit of 14 members and needs to be divided. Since the leader senses that some will feel bad about the separation, he divides the cell group "fairly" into equal halves by drawing lots and announces this as the only possible solution. The result: The group members rebel against the leader who now has to resort to his "God-given authority" to settle the conflict.

A church discovers that the longer members have been Christians, the fewer their contacts with non-Christians. Since the church puts a great value on friendship evangelism, all members are trained in building new friendships with non-Christians. At first everything goes according to plan. But soon reports about the frustration of more introverted Christians who feel like "total failures" in the business of building up new contacts.

At a youth retreat, a girl shares how difficult it is for her to have her devotional time right after getting up. Could she have her quiet time right after breakfast when she was more awake? The other group members nod understandingly, but the answer of the group leader is unmistakable: Jesus had His prayer time in the early morning, because after breakfast the day has already taken its course . . .

Exercise 12: Go through these examples and identify the following four aspects for each:

5. The intended goal of the action (in the first example: "more evangelistic activities".)

6. The opposing force that needs to be met (in the first example: "lack of evangelistic giftedness of some Christians.")

7. Energy used to overcome the opposing force (in the first example: "create feelings of guilt through appeals".)

8. The force that needs to be used to reach the real goal (in the first example: "Commitment to participate in evangelistic programs.")

Where Does the Wind Blow into Your Face?

The church that declares all Christians to be evangelists; the church that wants to hire a new staff member; the small group leader who divides his group, the leader of the youth retreat who praises the quietness of the morning—they all have something in common: All of them feel resistance to their work, a head wind blowing into their faces.

When you feel the wind blowing into your face as you minister, it could be that you are not yet applying the principle of energy transformation efficiently. Of course, this head wind could be caused by resistance that we are not at all responsible for. But it could also be that we are provoking resistance through the very steps we have taken to improve the growth of the church, but which contradict biotic principles. In both cases, you will have to learn how to turn resisting forces in the desired direction to accomplish the intended goal.

Exercise 13: Brainstorm a list of all those "head winds" which are blowing into your face in your ministry. Then think through which of these winds has been provoked by your own energies.

Resisting forces	Caused by yourself? How?
_____	_____
_____	_____
_____	_____
_____	_____
_____	_____
_____	_____
_____	_____

Exercise 14: Now try to categorize the resisting forces by grouping together those who have similar origins under a common heading. For instance: "Gift-orientation ignored" or "needs overlooked." In other words, what are the main causes of resistance in the church?

The Japanese sport of Jujitsu is quite different than boxing. Jujitsu goes back to Chinese marshal arts. About 1500 years ago, the monks of the monastery of Shanin had to resist numerous robbers. Since they were bound to a vow renouncing violence, they developed a set of "soft" fighting techniques that do not destroy the forces of the enemy; rather they redirect them through the use of a few leverage tricks. Besides just minimal steering energy which directs the strength of the opponent on himself, no other energy needs to be used to reach the desired goal.

Jujitsu Beats the Boxer Mentality

The biotic principle of energy transformation is based on the same insight. In ministry, we do not want to use twice as much energy as before (our resources of people, time, etc. are limited) but learn to use existing energies as wisely as possible. Our goal is to become like the surfer, who skillfully and with great speed (with only steering energy) glides through the waves, rather than the ocean liner that plows through the waves using enormous energy resources.

Some time ago, there was a great evangelistic campaign organized in several countries that targeted the mass mailing of an evangelistic brochure to every home. One of the churches in Southern Germany decided to participate, even though the church leadership, having learned about biotic principles, had misgivings about the effectiveness of this relatively expensive and impersonal form of evangelism.

But why did the church participate anyway? During the last few years church members had been led to develop *oikos-evangelism* using existing contacts with non-Christians and were eager after so much quiet (and successful) work to engage in something more visible and public. The pastor understood the dynamics and decided to use the existing motivations according to the principle of energy transformation.

Exercise 15: Look at the examples at the beginning of this chapter (pages 147-148): How could the resisting forces be transformed with just some steering energy to reach the desired goal in a better way?

Example	Energy Transformation
"Every Christian an evangelist"	Encourage gift discovery; free people with gift of evangelism of other tasks; encourage people with other gifts to use their gifts in evangelistic ministry
"Hiring a new staff member"	_____ _____
"Small group"	_____ _____
"Friendship evangelism"	_____ _____
"Personal devotions"	_____ _____

Using the Principle of Energy Transformation

Using the principle of energy transformation, work through the problems on page 129, then your own "live" example noted there.

Exercise 16: Read the two examples on page 129 and jot down your answers to the questions of Worksheet 5 (page 222, make a copy for each example). Then turn to the "live" example from your own church and apply the same questions. Finally, review the situation in Exercise 13 and try to find solutions that will transform existing opposing energies and not create new resistance.

Guiding Questions

1. *Which are the opposing forces that you need to deal with in this problem? How could they be meaningfully "transformed"?*

2. *Evaluate the elements of the solutions developed in the preceding two chapters then ask if any of them might generate resistance. How could this be avoided? (This part of the exercise is not applicable to Exercise 13.)*

3. *Now go through all your ideas for energy transformation: Have you carefully made sure to avoid any of the main sources of resistance (see Exercise 14)?*

This Is How You Could Have Proceeded

On the following page you will find our thoughts on Example 2. You will notice that any of the solutions discussed so far, even those based on biotic principles, could—but not necessarily would—cause resistance. For this reason it is important to realize that all six biotic principles work synergistically together. The isolated application of one principle suggested here facilitates our study of each of the principles, but it is, strictly speaking, a technocratic approach. To balance our approach we will combine all six principles in Training Unit 7.

Our solution deals with steps that were developed from the perspectives of interdependence and multiplication. You may have found other areas where resistance could develop. Evaluate the elements of the solutions you have developed in the preceding training units to see if any of them could generate opposing forces. How could they be prevented?

Exercise 11: Using Worksheet 3 (page 220) take at least fifteen minutes to reflect on your own thought process as you found solutions to Exercise 16.

Reflect on Your Ideas

Part 4:
Learning to think
biotically

Worksheet: Energy Transformation in Action

Step	Possible resistance	Energy transformation
A pastoral meeting with the pastor	No readiness; suspects it is church discipline	Clarify as an offer for help
Find new team member	Current worker reacts as though hurt	Gaining perspective through periodic rest from work
Prayer team intercedes for marriage	Fear of indiscreet leak	Make sure there is absolute confidentiality
Leaders who also care for personal life concerns	Suspects meddling with personal life	Emphasize holistic character of help
Small group takes up spiritual challenge	Small group pressures for responsibility	Experience support as actual help
Friends live relationships	Reserve because of insecurity	Motivate those able to have relationships. Sweep "insecure ones" along.
Worker will lead a self-help group	Not his gift	Share experiences in a way that corresponds with his gifts

Suggestions for Group Learning

Remember the guidelines for group exercises already mentioned in the preceding chapters:

1. Before you conduct the exercises, group members need a basic knowledge of energy transformation.

2. Use images, pictures, and stories when you explain the principle of energy transformation to your group members and watch for those "aha" effects.

3. Begin always with an easy exercise.

4. During each exercise, plan enough time for evaluation.

Introduction

Explain the principle of energy transformation to your group. As an illustration, you could describe the difference between boxing and Ju-jitsu. As an introduction to the first exercise, present the examples listed in the main text of this chapter.

Instructions to Exercise 12 and 15

Divide the total group into several subgroups of three to five persons. Each subgroup works on one of the mentioned examples on pages 147-148 using the questions of Exercise 12. If you have more than twenty persons in your group, you will have some groups working on the same example. If you have less than twelve participants, groups may have more than one example to deal with. Ask all participants to jot down the results of their discussion.

After some ten to fifteen minutes, build new groups with a representative from each original group in each of the new groups. If you had five groups with three participants you will end up now with three groups with five members. In these new groups each representative of the five examples presents the results and reports about the discussion in their groups. Thus there is no need for a plenary session.

Exercise 15 should follow immediately after Exercise 12. Ask participants to go back to their original groups. Let them discuss how the forces of resistance can be transformed through using some steering energy. This time, have groups present their findings in the plenary group.

Instructions to Exercise 13 and 14

Exercises 13 and 14 should be conducted differently in a group setting. First, through brainstorming, develop a list of situations where resisting forces in your church become visible (which in some cases might be responsible for some unsuccessful church growth measures). These could be examples which concern the whole church, or examples from the specific ministry areas your group members are working in. After the brainstorming session, divide the group into subgroups of three. Each subgroup selects one or two of the listed situations. They will think through which forces were operating in the specific situation. Use the following steps:

1. On a blank sheet of paper, divide the page into two columns by drawing a vertical line in the middle of the paper.

2. On the left side, list all the forces that were favorable to the goal in this situation.

3. On the right side of the paper, write all the forces that work against the goal.

4. Now draw arrows pointing towards the middle line for each item. Let the thickness and the length of the arrow indicate the strength of the forces.

5. Such forces and counter forces can be: people, values, structures and programs, contextual factors, crises, knowledge, ideas, advantages, traditions, gifts, and needs.

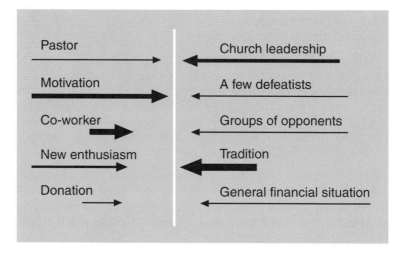

6. Think it through with your group: Are these forces of resistance self-made and provoked by in-house factors? What categories do these causes belong to? Can we see any headings using natural church development thinking like "ignores gift-based approach," "overlooks needs," etc.?

In the end, the groups share their results with the whole group.

Instructions to Exercise 16 Since you probably won't have enough time to work through all the examples in the group (the two we presented and those you presented in Exercise 13), decide which ones you want to work on. If you used the examples of Exercise 16 in the other training units, it might be interesting to use them here also. You can also continue with Exercise 13. In this case you will only do part one of the exercise.

An alternative might be to have two subgroups working on different examples.

Build groups of five who discuss the examples and identify possible forces of resistance, and opportunities for energy transformation. Give at least fifteen minutes per example.

You can conduct this exercise after any of the exercises in this training unit to complete and reinforce the subject. Ask each participant to work individually through the questions of the worksheet.

Instructions to Exercise 17

After fifteen minutes, participants are asked to share their thoughts in groups of three. Each triad is asked to make a list of successful and unsuccessful thought strategies with which all participants can identify (even if they have not applied them themselves). The lists are then presented to the whole group.

Training Unit 4: Multi-usage

"According to our experience, the principle of multi-usage is the stepchild of all biotic principles."

Test question: Do the results of this measure further sustain this ministry, or do we have here only a one-way street? See NCD, pages 72-73

"Multi-usage? Yes, we have used that principle for a long time in our church," said the pastor when we mentioned this principle to him. "Recently we bought a keyboard which now serves the praise team, the choir and the evangelism team. This investment has been worth far more than we paid for it. When we bought our overhead projector we thought along similar lines. . ."

Is this multi-usage? The fourth biotic principle is, in our experience, the real stepchild of all six principles. It is usually only given attention in a relatively shallow way, as in the example above. But at the core of this principle we look for something else, namely, "Does this measure lead to positive results that further reinforce this measure? Is this measure part of the biotic cycle?"

To understand this principle, one has to think "around the corner." Many people have some difficulties thinking in such relatively complex relationships. Linear and mono-causal thinking is much simpler to understand.

Financial One-way Streets

When we are invited by churches to conduct a seminar about natural church development, we encounter a range of possible ways to finance the costs of such a seminar. Most often a church will pay the costs from local church funds so that all participants can be there for free. Sometimes a church will ask for an offering to cover at least part of the costs of the "free" seminar. But in order to raise the funds for the seminar, the church must usually invest quite an effort: proposals to higher denominational entities, negotiations for an account for church development in the yearly budget, or more appeals for funds to refill exhausted financial reserves.

Instead of a cyclical process, churches often use a one-way street approach. They have to first invest energy to motivate persons to participate in the seminar and to organize the event. Then they have to invest energy into fund-raising. This means double work without cross-pollination. Often, such church-sponsored, paid seminars are filled with persons who are eager to volunteer their opinions but who really lack the motivation to get involved in the continued development of the church.

What would a multi-usage cycle look like? First, those who profit from the seminar participate in financing it. When seminar participants pay a seminar fee, the same energy that is directed towards the preparation and conducting of the seminar also provides its financial backing. Thus the seminar is financially self-supporting without creating additional burdens. In addition, paying participants are better motivated than non-paying ones. (Of course, the church will help pay for those who are unable to pay.)

Evangelistic One-way Streets

Many churches invest a considerable part of their energy into evangelistic work. In looking at their approaches, we often observe one-way streets. They train members in how to win people for Christ, form small groups, and organize classes for new believers. These activities can be meaningful, but sometimes, leaders fail to think about how to use invested energies in multiple ways so that the results of individual actions (new converts) flow back to benefit future evangelistic work.

How could that happen? If those who are led to Christ could be helped to share their faith with their friends and relatives and help them believe in Christ, the energy cycle would be closed. Thus, the results of evangelism would flow into maintaining and expanding the evangelistic activities of the church continuously.

Pastoral One-way Streets

Similar interrelationships can also be observed in the area of pastoral counseling. The few counselors in the church are visited by new people seeking help. After they have been helped, they merge back into their normal church life. Energy was invested to help these persons. But energy has to also be invested to keep up the counseling ministry: counselors have to be identified (according to their spiritual gifts) and trained, (using the apprenticeship or co-leadership principle). If some of those seeking help, after they have been helped, could be trained to create a self-help group for "their" concern, the energy cycle would be closed. The same energy that provided pastoral help in counseling contributes now to maintain and expand this ministry.

One-way Streets in Leadership Development

The expression "co-leadership" or "apprenticeship principle" leads to another area that illustrates the meaning of multi-usage. Today we often approach leadership training from a program oriented paradigm. Churches offer seminars and instruction to train leaders; if a church does not have enough capacity to do it herself, Bible institutes may help. In this approach, energy has to be continually invested to train new leaders. However, the fruit of this energy investment (the new leaders) does not contribute to maintaining the training process, and certainly not to its expansion. As soon as each leader is also responsible for training and coaching an apprentice on the job, a multi-usage cycle is in operation.

Whenever the church organizes events where persons provide help or training for others, who then are free to just "consume" it without contributing something back into the system, a natural cycle is severed. The body of Christ is built on the principle of mutuality and reciprocal service. Instead of being consumers, church members need to be empowered to contribute to the life of the church. This is multi-usage in action.

Exercise 18: Evaluate the different programs and activities of your church from the perspective of the principle of multi-usage. Do this by trying to insert the selected activity or program into a cyclical figure as we have done in the first illustration. Is this possible? Or is the positive feedback lacking that is necessary to maintain and expand the ministry?

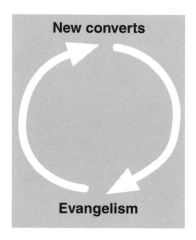

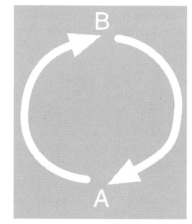

How Do You Create Multi-usage? What practical steps can you take to transform a current "one-way activity" (possibly one you identified in Exercise 18) into a program with multi-usage benefits? Or how do you design new ministries with built-in multi-usage dimensions?

The obvious, but not very systematic, solution is to evaluate each project as you did in Exercise 18. When you find an alternative that meets the criteria of multi-usage you have arrived at your goal. The problem with this approach is that it usually only works for people with the intuitive ability to arrive at solutions with multi-usage benefits. If you want to find a solution systematically, proceed through the following four steps.

Step 1: Separate the Individual Steps in the Cycle If you already had a cycle in mind, you would already have the solution! If not, limit yourself in this first step to looking at the first half of the cycle. At this stage define: What is your starting point? What is the intended goal? Let's use the example we used above to illustrate this process:

- Church growth seminar: The starting point is a seminar in natural church development. The intended goal is workers who are trained and motivated for their ministry in the church.

- Evangelism: The starting point is evangelistic activities. The intended goal is to see people make a new decision for a life with Christ.

- Counseling: The starting point are people who need help. The intended result is people who have found inner healing.

This first step can be illustrated graphically this way:

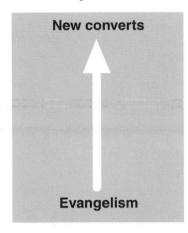

This step comes easy for most people. It conforms to the typical, non-biotic linear way of thinking. Yet it provides the point of departure for a solution characterized by multi-usage benefits.

Important: Do not yet start to think about *how* to reach the intended goal. At this stage just define the two stations—starting point and goal—as clearly as possible.

Exercise 19: For the example "leadership development" proceed the same way we demonstrated with the other examples. Define the starting point and the intended goal and write them into the graphic to the left.

Step Two: Create a second "one-way street."

Since it is easier for most of us to find a linear "one-way" solution than a complete cycle we should use this tendency to our advantage. In the second step, the goal is to find a solution whose result can have a positive feedback on the starting point. Notice that you are merely exchanging roles for starting position and intended result. You now see that the most important difference between a non-biotic solution and one that aims at multi-usage benefits is the way we think about solutions. Biotic solutions anticipate the next step and thus think one step further ahead! Let us take another look at the three examples mentioned before:

Step 2: Create a Second "One-way Street"

- Seminar: Starting point is the workers who will visit the seminar. The intended result is the implementation (financing included) of the seminar.

- Evangelism: Starting point is now the people who will become believers. The intended result is that there will be more evangelism in the church.

- Pastoral care: Starting point is now the people who have been helped through counseling. The intended result is that other persons with problems may find help through pastoral care.

The figure would now look like the following:

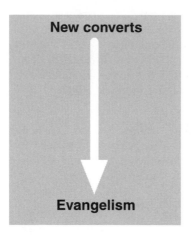

Exercise 20: Try step two for the example "leadership development." Write your answers in the right side of the graphic above.

Step 3: Develop a Plan How to Implement Step 2.

The particularly new aspect of this step is not the way you plan the implementation of step 2, but rather the fact that you are focusing on implementing step 2 before you have thought more about step 1. Proceed as you usually do when you are planning an activity—hopefully you are keeping in mind biotic principles.

- Seminar: If those participating at the seminar are expected to be the solution for financing the seminar, it is obvious that a participation fee must be charged.

- Evangelism: If the newly converted are to be the key for more evangelism in the church, it makes sense for them to be trained in sharing their faith.

- Pastoral care: If the persons who have been helped are to contribute to helping other persons finding pastoral care as well, think about ways to use those who have been helped, according to their gifts. For example: as lay counselors, as leaders of self-help groups, as Christians who encourage others through their testimony, etc.

Exercise 21: How could example "leadership development" be implemented? Try your own solution:

_____

_____

_____

_____

_____

_____

_____

Step 4: Develop a plan to implement step 1.

Step 4: Now Focus on Step 1

The solution for step 1 will be obvious if you have followed the instructions for the other steps. Remember, step 1 is dependent on the realization of step 2 and not the other way around. For our three examples this means:

- Seminar: If the seminar will be financed through participant fees, this must be accounted for in the planning and preparation process. The church must calculate the costs, accurately estimate how many participants can be expected, indicate the seminar fee in the seminar brochure, directly contact prospective participants and motivate them to participate, etc.

- Evangelism: If new converts are to be trained in how to share their new faith in Christ, the church must encourage structures to help Christians reach out to their *oikos* network. Increased evangelistic activities should therefore aim at strengthening relationships, and be more gift-based and need-oriented. The problem with conventional evangelistic approaches is that people who have been won that way have a harder time beginning *oikos*-evangelistic sharing than people who have found Christ through Christians in their network of friends in the first place.

- Pastoral Care: Train your counselors to keep their eyes open for potential counselors or persons who can share their personal experiences among those who have received help through their ministry.

Exercise 22: *Write out a plan for implementing step 1 for the example "leadership development" (you can follow the model of example "pastoral care"):*

_____

_____

_____

_____

_____

_____

_____

_____

Here is a summary of exercises 19-22:

• Step 1: Starting point is "the necessity for new workers." The expected result is "increase the number of leaders who have received minimum training."

• Step 2: The starting point is "a group of trained new workers," the expected result is "more trained leaders."

• Step 3: If leaders are to bring forth more leaders, on-the-job training models must be considered.

• Step 4: More trained workers will result from training new leaders in the skills for their new ministry and in the art of spotting and developing new coworkers. This approach should become part of the genetic code of new leaders.

Applying the Principle of Multi-usage

The traditional approach to find solutions for the mentioned examples looks like this: One finds a solution for step 1 in the problem concerned, then develops solutions to the other problems created by the solution! Our approach distinguishes itself clearly: After identifying step 1, we do not immediately look for a solution to the problem, but rather address step 2. Only after finding a satisfying solution for step 2 do we come back to solve step 1, depending on the solution found in step 2.

Exercise 23: *Read again the case studies on page 129 and note your answers to the questions on Worksheet 6 (page 223, please copy one time for each example). Then address the example from your church that you selected on page 129.*

For each example follow all four steps consecutively:

- Step 1: What is the starting point? What is the intended goal?

- Step 2: What is the starting point here? What is the intended goal here?

- Step 3: How could step 2 be implemented?

- Step 4: How can step 1 be realized, considering the solution found in step 2?

Here's how we might approach case study 2, taking into account the principle of multi-usage. This case, which at first does not seem to have much to do with church development, is an interesting example of the effects of this principle.

A Possible Approach

Step 1: What is the starting point? Step 2: What is the starting point
What is the intended goal?   here? What is the intended goal here?

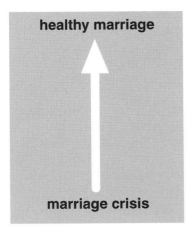

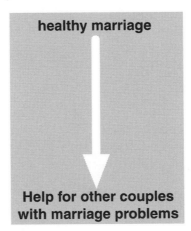

Step 3: How could step 2 be implemented?

As mentioned in the "pastoral care" example, there are several possibilities to implement step 2. If the pastoral care process has led to a restoration of the marriage relationship, the couple could be invited to share their healing experience during the worship service. Perhaps the two could lead a self-help group for couples, or at least become part of the team. And—if they have the right gift mix—their participation in the pastoral care ministry of the church would also be an option.

Please note: In some situations, none of the solutions mentioned here can be applied. However, it does make a great difference for the long-term development of the pastoral care ministry in the church if such solutions are at least borne in mind, rather than never considered in the first place.

Step 4: How can step 1 be realized considering the solution found in step 2?

Reflect on Your Ideas

In step 1, the goal is to help people in a marriage crisis find healing for their marriage. In step 2 the goal is that the capacity of the church to minister to people in crisis will expand (in different ways) through people who have at one point benefited from this ministry. The solution is not just to focus on step 1, (to restore the marriage of the couple in crisis), but to also consider how this couple can possibly minister later to others. For this reason, those working in the pastoral care ministry of the church have to be trained not only in how to minister to people through caring, but in recruiting new members for their ministry team.

Here we want to again evaluate the preceding exercise by reflecting on our own thought process. How did you find solutions to Exercise 23? What thought strategies did you use? How did you work over and improve your solution, maybe even after you read our suggested solution?

Exercise 24: Using Worksheet 3 (page 220) take at least fifteen minutes to reflect on your own thought process as you found solutions to Exercise 23.

Suggestions for Group Learning

Remember the guidelines for group exercises already mentioned in the preceding chapters:

1. Before you conduct the exercises, the group members should have a basic knowledge of multi-usage.

2. Use images, pictures, and stories when you explain the principle of multi-usage to your group members and watch for those "aha" effects.

3. Always begin with an easy exercise.

4. During each exercise, plan enough time for evaluation.

Introduction

Present the principle of multi-usage in your own words to your group. A useful illustration is the example in *Natural Church Development*, page 72: the leaves that fall from a tree turn into humus and provide nutrients to support the further growth of the tree from which they fell. In this example, the principle of multi-usage is discernible as a cycle: Humus furthers the growth of the tree, including its new leaves; those leaves turn into humus again, thus completing the cycle.

After this introduction, carefully present the examples found in this chapter (pages 156-158).

Instructions to Exercise 18

Draw the cycle illustration with the pole A and B on a blackboard or flip chart so that the participants have this interrelationship clearly before their eyes. (An alternative would be to work from an overhead slide or with worksheet handouts.)

Ask participants to divide into groups of three, then look at any areas of the church, (preaching ministry, small group ministry, training of team members, etc.): Is there any cyclical multi-usage effect visible? Indicate that the goal is not to find any solutions but to diagnose situations. Have the groups present their ideas to the plenary group and discuss them.

Instructions to Exercises 19-23

Exercise 23 is really a summary of exercises 19-22, only with different examples. No matter which examples you want to use, you can proceed in your group according to the following instructions. Probably the most helpful way to proceed is to use the examples of exercise 23 (or only a selection) to ensure you have worked at least completely through one example using all biotic principles.

1. Divide into groups of three but keep all participants in the same room so they can hear your instructions and comments. For each example, each participant receives a copy of Worksheet 6 (page 223).

2. Present step 1—including the examples given in the text. Make sure all participants understand their task. Then let them do the exercise for step 1.

3. After about ten minutes let each group of three present its solutions to the other groups. Take some time to discuss the ideas presented and learn from one another.

4. Repeat the same process for steps 2 to 4: Explain the step concerned. Give time for questions of clarification. Then let them work in their groups and share the results with the other groups.

This exercise is not done in one "trip" but step by step as in exercises 19-22.

Instructions to Exercise 24

Ask each participant to work individually through the questions of the worksheet. After fifteen minutes, have participants share their thoughts in groups of three. Each triad is asked to make a list of successful and unsuccessful thought strategies with which all participants can identify (even if they have not applied them themselves). The lists are then presented to the whole group.

Training Unit 5: Symbiosis

Test question: Does this step contribute to fruitful coopera- tion of different forms of ministry, or does it promote an ecclesiastic mono-culture?

See NCD, pages 74-75

"The church can function according to God's plan only as it lives symbiotically."

There are trees that are so old that they are unable to absorb the life sustaining nutrients from the ground. Their roots no longer have the fine endings. Such trees would be con- demned to die if there were not those special kinds of fungus that spawn around the too bulky tree roots and deliver the nutrients. The delivery is however not totally "free of charge," because the fungus- es have their own problem. Since they do not produce chlorophyll, they lack the ability to convert carbon dioxide and water into carbo- hydrates and oxygen.

It is only in this form that plants can do anything with these nutri- ents. Consequently the fungus receives back from the tree part of the nutrients but in modified form. This arrangement of life profiting from each other biologists call "symbiosis." Both parts benefit from it. Indeed in many cases both of their existences are made possible only in this way.

The principle of symbiosis is described over and over again in the Bible. Perhaps the most striking example is Paul's explanation of how the body of Christ, the church, functions: "If the whole body were an eye, where would the sense of hearing be? If the whole body were an ear where would the sense of smell be? But in fact God has arranged the parts in the body, every one of them, just as he wanted them to be. If they were all one part, where would the body be? As it is, there are many parts, but one body. The eye cannot say to the hand, 'I don't need you!' and the head cannot say to the feet, 'I don't need you!'" (1. Cor. 12:17-21). Mutual complementation, mutual depen- dence, mutual benefit, diversity in unity— these are the key words that translate the term "symbiosis" into a language we Christians are probably more familiar with.

Diversity in Unity

The church can function according to God's plan only as it lives in symbiosis—as one body with many mutually complementing mem- bers. Thus wherever the biotic principle of symbiosis is ignored, the body suffers.

The quality characteristic that most obviously reflects the meaning of symbiosis is the factor of "gift-oriented ministry." Christians exhibit an enormous diversity, since every person possesses a different gift mix. In this diversity they work together and enrich each other. One

One Body, Many Members, Many Gifts

person has the gift of hospitality and offers comfortable and warm-hearted fellowship to a small group. Someone has the gift of teaching and helps the participants of the group to focus on biblical principles and reflect on them. Someone has the gift of music and leads the group into a time of worship through songs. Someone else has the gift of counseling and the group benefits from it. Someone else has the gift of helps and supports the host in her preparations.

The same principle of mutual complementation not only applies to individual Christians, but also to diverse groups and forms of ministry. Just recently we encountered a beautiful example of this. A small-group coordinator discovered the need in his church to not only have their regular small groups, but also to offer small groups with a pastoral ministry focus. Instead of initiating such groups himself, he contacted the director of their pastoral ministry. As they discussed the need and worked together using their own giftedness and strengths to complement each other, a new branch of pastoral ministry that was also part of the small-group ministry of the church developed.

Condition: Diversity

Complementation is only possible where there is diversity. The test question at the beginning of this chapter points to the greatest enemy of any symbiosis—mono-culture, the inner-church or even inter-church "template Christianity." Many Christians wish for a uniform cell group with exactly prescribed standard programs that are mandatory for all groups of the church and use the argument that Christ wants unity in His church. Others desire the "unity" of all Christians. They urge all churches in a local area to "become one" in the sense of being more uniform. They also feel that a church should not pick a certain ministry focus group, but be there "for everybody." This approach is a deeply technocratic concept of unity which makes cross-fertilization among diverse parts almost impossible by substituting mono-culture for diversity, and uniformity for spiritual unity.

Exercise 25: Where in your church do you find tendencies towards uniformity? Can you find examples like the standardized small group mentioned above? Think through all the areas of ministry in your church, for instance, the training of leaders, worship service, children's ministry, lay counseling, etc.

_____

_____

_____

_____

The term "diversity" does not have a positive ring for every Christian. For some it smacks of competition and of the danger of separatism. Differences can be threatening (just think of the causes of animosity against foreigners). Churches with different styles of expressing their spirituality isolate themselves more rapidly than those who have the same "body odor." People who find a liking to each other like to spend time together and work together better than those who consider themselves only "brothers and sisters"—the motto there is: "You can choose your friends but you're stuck with your brothers and sisters." The director of the small-group ministry who wants to introduce new types of groups can count on reactions like: "What will we do if some of our small-group members finds a better group and wants to leave ours?" Diversity also produces fear!

Diversity Yes—Competition No!

Exercise 26: Where in your church can you find feelings of competition? Look at the different areas of ministry in your church and describe some concrete examples.

_____

_____

_____

_____

Every church is comprised of diversity of people, the real question is how we deal with it: Do we press everybody into the same mold? Do we foster competition? Or do we encourage cooperation and complementation? The choice is yours. Symbiosis is therefore one of three possible choices as we deal with the God-given diversity in the church. It is also the exact opposite of either uniformity or competition.

The Choice Is Yours!

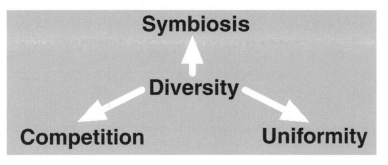

When we insist on uniformity we make it impossible that every Christian can participate in ministry according to his or her personality and gifts as God intended it for him or her. Moreover Christians do not receive the blessings of service to them in the church and through the church in harmony with God's will. Uniformity thus contradicts the character of the body of Christ.

Competitive thinking, on the other hand, invests a lot of energy into staying away from others or even fighting them. This energy would be better used to work together for a common goal. It leads to ignoring "weaker members" or pushing them against the wall instead of recognizing their important function in the total organism and treating them "with special honor" (1 Cor. 12:23). Competition also contradicts the character of the body of Christ.

Symbiosis, by contrast, leads to cross-fertilization ("win-win situation"): Small groups in the church that do not hover over their members and act in competition to other groups, but instead help church members to find the group that will best fit their needs and help them to grow spiritually ("win" number one). When a group has members who feel comfortable there and see they fit in, the whole group benefits (second "win").

Exercise 27: Look at the examples of uniformity and competition you identified in the exercises above. What consequences can you see? How would symbiosis work here? What would be its consequences?

Your Example	Consequences	Symbiosis	Consequences

Utilizing the Principle of Symbiosis

Now we will again work through the three problems described on page 129. We have already worked on them in the last few chapters, but this time, we will address them from the perspective of the principle of symbiosis.

Exercise 28: Read again through the two examples on page 129 and write down your answers to the questions on worksheet 7 (page 224; please make a copy for each of the examples). Then do the same exercise also for the example from your church that you selected on page 129.

Work through each example using the following questions:

1. When you look at your solutions suggested in previous chapters: Are there any traces of "uniformity" in your own solutions?

2. What would uniformity look like apart from your own solution? How could it be avoided?

3. Is there any danger of competition in any of your suggested solutions? Where?

4. What would competition look like apart from your own solution? How could it be avoided?

5. What symbiotic elements could be incorporated into a solution?

Here is an illustration for applying the principle of symbiosis using example 2.

Uniformity could have a role here in several ways:

- If the leader worked in children's ministry despite a lack of giftedness in this area ("Anybody can do that!").

- If the small group of this leader could not meet his needs and help him in his marriage crisis because there are only standard groups with a uniform program ("Singing, praying, Bible reading, singing, praying, end").

- If a counselor offers only well meaning advice that fits neither his situation nor his personality ("Why don't you try my pair of glasses, they really helped me.")

These tendencies could be avoided through gift-oriented ministry, diversity in the small-group ministry ("holistic small groups") and active listening.

Competition could play a role in the following points:

- If the leader wants to hold on to his work in children's ministry at any cost, and feels threatened by the thought of turning over this work to someone else.

- If the counselor, pastor, small-group leader, or friends of this leader would all think they alone could help him better than anybody else.

- If some of those identified for a gift-oriented solution insist on special treatment or engaging in "gift projection."

- If the solution that encourages diversity among small groups is based on a relationship of competition among the groups.

The following "symbiotic elements" could be incorporated into the solution:

- Gift-oriented ministry in order to prevent burn-out and the resulting problems.

- Holistic small groups (some thematic groups focusing on the theme of "marriage"), in order to meet needs and minister to actual problems.

- Training of counselors in how to recognize individual differences in those seeking counsel and how not to treat each person with a standard solution.

- Training for teams and leaders stressing teamwork and discouraging competition.

Reflect on Your Ideas Here we want to again evaluate the preceding exercise by reflecting on our own ideas. How did you find solutions to this exercise? What thought strategies did you use? How did you work over and improve your solution, maybe even after you read our suggested solution?

Exercise 29: Using Worksheet 3 (page 220), take at least fifteen minutes to reflect on your own thought process as you found solutions to Exercise 28.

Suggestions for Group Learning

Again remember the guidelines for group exercises already mentioned in the preceding chapters:

1. Before you conduct the exercises, the group members should have a basic knowledge of symbiosis.

2. Use images, pictures, and stories when you explain the principle of symbiosis to your group members and watch for those "aha" effects.

3. Always begin with an easy exercise.

4. During each exercise, plan enough time for evaluation.

Introduction

Create a sensibility for individuality and diversity among the participants by conducting the game "Tohuwabohu" (see Worksheet 8, page 225). Each participant receives a copy of the worksheet with the instruction to collect as many signatures from other participants as possible within the next ten minutes. Other participants can sign each statement that applies to them.

After the game ask who has collected the most signatures. Ask some of the participants how many different signatures they received. Was any one person able to sign all the lines? Why not?

By the way, the statements are taken from the questionnaire of the "gift test" and indicate the various gifts of persons. The game is thus an important indication that everybody is different, has special gifts that need the complementation of others if the church of Christ is to function as the body of Christ.

**Instructions to
Exercise 25**

Before you conduct exercise 25, please summarize in your own words the content of this chapter. Then through brainstorming, try to identify examples of uniformity in your church (depending on the size of the group use subgroups or the plenary group).

**Instructions to
Exercise 26**

In your group discuss what kind of fears can be generated by diversity in a church. If the discussion slows down you can nurture it through examples from the section "Diversity, yes—competition, no!" Symbiosis as an alternative to competition must be nurtured by a sense of cooperation and teamwork. To encourage a sense of teamwork you might want to conduct the following exercise:

First build groups of five and seat each team around a table. In addition there is at least one observer per group who will watch the behavior of the participants and make sure that the rules are obeyed. On each table there will be a big manila envelope containing five smaller envelopes with the material for the game. These envelopes are marked with the letter A, B, C, D, and E. In the envelopes are the parts of a square (see illustration) in the following content:

Envelope A: Pieces I, H, and E
Envelope B: Pieces A, A, A, and C
Envelope C: Pieces A and J
Envelope D: Pieces D and F
Envelope E: Pieces G, B, F, and C

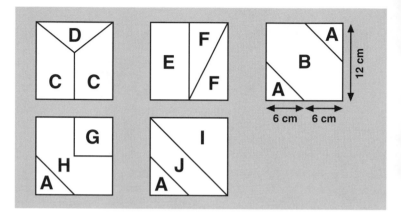

The objective of this game is to develop the solution as a team since one cannot be found individually. An enclosed sheet will contain the following instructions: "The envelope on the table contains five other envelopes with pieces from which you are to form squares. As soon as you hear the starting signal each group is to make five squares of exactly the same size. The task is not over until all participants have built a square of identical proportions in front of them."

During the exercise there are the following rules:

1. None of the players is allowed to speak.

2. None of the players is allowed to ask for a piece or signal that a certain piece is needed or should be given to him/her by someone else.

3. Every player may voluntarily give up pieces and put it into the center of the table or hand it to another player, but no player is allowed to directly touch the figure of another.

4. Any player can take a piece from the center of the table, but no one is allowed to build in the center of the table.

5. After the director has explained the rules of the game and instructed all participants in their task, one of the group members opens the big envelope and hands the participants one of the envelopes A-E. At the signal of the observers the game starts, the participants open their envelopes and the observers start the stopwatch.

6. During the game several things become clear: If after a certain orientation time the group does not develop a mode of cooperation it is impossible to accomplish the task. Sometimes the game facilitates very intense emotions. How does one feel when it is impos-

sible to proceed alone? When one has to depend on someone else? When one cannot help someone else directly? When a player holds on to an important piece without realizing that he holds the key to the solution in his own hand? What feelings arise towards those who are slower?

7. Evaluate this exercise in a thorough discussion in which both observers and players share their experiences.

Instructions to Exercise 28

Since you may not have enough time to work through all the examples (the lesson examples and your own church based one) in your group you should first decide which ones you will actually work on. If you as a group have already worked on any of the examples for the other biotic principles it might be interesting to use them now as well. An alternative approach would be to let different subgroups work on different examples. Each participant should get a copy of Worksheet 7 (page 224) for the selected example and work on it at first individually. The solutions found are then discussed in groups of three and finally shared in the plenary group.

Instructions to Exercise 29

Instruct participants to fill out the questions of the evaluation sheet, at first, individually. After fifteen minutes, ask them to share their thoughts in groups of three. Each triad is asked to make a list of successful and unsuccessful thought strategies with which all participants can identify (even if they have not applied them themselves). The lists are then presented to the whole group.

Training Unit 6: Functionality

*"What once
used to be
quite functional
can easily
become some-
thing rather
strange."*

Test question: Is this measure producing fruit for the king-dom of God, or is it missing its purpose? See NCD, pages 76-77

A girl once asked her mother: "Why do you always cut the end of the roast, then lay that end on top before you put it into the oven?" The mother thought for a moment only to admit: "I learned that from your grandmother. I don't know why she did that. But I will ask her." A short time later her opportunity came. "Tell me why did you always cut the end of the roast and lay that end on top of the roast before putting it into the oven?" The grandmother answered: "Don't you remember how small our oven was? That big Sunday roast just did not fit in one piece."

Some things are quite meaningful and appropriate, that is, function-al, at a certain point in time. But when the situation changes (and our behavior does not change at the same time) the formerly functional can rapidly develop into something anachronistic or even strange.

Our churches suffer from both: structures, activities, and measures that were meaningful earlier but are no longer because the situation has changed. At the same time there are structures, activities, and measures that have never been functional because they were designed from the beginning in such a way that they never could be fruitful. There are many other motivations than that of developing a living church organism that can play a role in the development of structures: traditionalism, fear of change, power needs, false theolog-ical paradigms, consumer attitudes, etc.

Evaluate Existing Programs

Imagine your church opens a Christian Café. Two years later you want to examine the effectiveness of this ministry. So you ask the members of the team: "How many guests are coming to the Café? Those who come, are they predominantly Christians or are there also persons with little Christian background? Do you lead evangelistic conversations?" The team members all agree: The Café is well attend-ed—by Christians of churches in the area and from your own church. Would this result bring you frustration or joy? Should this ministry continue on or be dropped? Are there any changes necessary or could it continue the old way?

How we evaluate this ministry depends totally on our criteria. If the Café was opened with the goal of encouraging the relationships among local Christians, then this ministry seems quite effective. But if it was founded to reach non-Christians, it is a total flop.

Those truly functional structures do not exist. Functionality depends on the criteria we apply. Spiritual fruit is the most important criterion of the biotic principle of functionality. Does this step contribute visible and measurable fruit for the development of the church? Qualitatively as well as quantitatively? Does this measure contribute to the improvement of the quality of our church (as indicated by the eight quality characteristics)? And does it help our church grow quantitatively or by multiplication?

Step 1: Define spiritual criteria.

Define Criteria

Using our example of the Christian Café this would mean that both goals, reaching non-Christians or furthering relationships, could help improve the quality of the church. One goal is a quality characteristic in the area of "need-oriented evangelism," the other refers to the quality characteristic "loving relationships." Notice that both goals positively impact the quantitative growth of the church—directly or indirectly. However, we should be careful not to declare the quality characteristics "loving relationships" afterwards as having been the goal of the Café ministry when the original goal was evangelism!

Exercise 30: *Make a list of a few of the ministries of your church. In the second column, write the success criterion for each ministry. Consider the goals of each ministry and make sure your criteria do not contradict biotic principles.*

Ministry	Success Criterion
_____	_____
_____	_____
_____	_____
_____	_____
_____	_____
_____	_____
_____	_____

Step 2: Evaluate the effectiveness of your ministries based on the criteria you defined.

Monitor Effectiveness

The question remains: Does the "Christian Café" represent the best possible means to reach the goal of the church (whatever that might be). This question should really be asked before the ministry is launched. But already existing ministries—whatever the reason and the circumstances for their existence—should be evaluated regularly for evidence of "fruit." For example, "Do unchurched people come to the Café and in this way find access to Christ and the church?" This would be the evaluation question if the Café was opened for the purpose of reaching the unchurched. Otherwise the question could have been: "Does the Café contribute to the deepening of relationships among Christians?"

Exercise 31: Go through the list of exercise 30: Which ministries can be considered functional and therefore successful in view of biotic criteria? Which are not? Mark the functional ministries with a check mark.

Overhaul Your "Ministry Menu"

Step 3: Revise or drop non-functional ministries.

If you have placed a check mark in front of all the ministries on your list you can skip step 3. But what do you do if you discover that an activity has to be viewed as a failure or at least a partial failure? If the Café was opened to reach unchurched people, but only Christians show up, you have two possibilities. You can drop such programs without replacement or replace with new, more effective ones. Or you can overhaul them, then after some time, examine the criteria again. In certain situations you may even change the goals and leave the activities unchanged. In the case of the Café, this would be appropriate if you have had a dream for a long time to do something to deepen the relationships between Christians—and here you have "accidentally" discovered a ministry that fulfills this purpose. But if you do this you should be highly self-critical. To justify the effectiveness of a inter-denominational evangelistic program, that did not facilitate the conversion of anybody, as a means of improving relationships between different churches would be too much self-justification.

Exercise 32: Those activities in exercise 31 that have not received a check mark should be dropped. Why? Which ones should continue, but in revised form? What would have to be changed?

Programs that should be dropped   **Reason**

_____	_____
_____	_____
_____	_____
_____	_____
_____	_____
_____	_____

Programs that should be modified	Kind of modification
_____	_____
_____	_____
_____	_____
_____	_____
_____	_____
_____	_____
_____	_____

Creating New Functional Programs

Perhaps you have noticed that it is not easy to evaluate the effectiveness of existing programs if you have not thought about the criteria for measuring effectiveness at the time of its introduction. The process of monitoring effectiveness starts before a new ministry is born. This does not mean that criteria once established cannot be changed. But it has to happen consciously and with reflection, by assigning new functional criteria, or we are lying to ourselves.

The following steps can help you plan new church programs in such a way that effectiveness can be monitored.

Step 1: Develop activities on the basis of real needs.

Create Need-Oriented Programs

A church consists of people who are different and have a diversity of needs. Therefore it is important that you ask yourself which of the needs of a certain ministry focus group you want to meet through any particular ministry. Programs that ignore the needs of people can only be maintained through appeals to their guilt. They tend to disappoint those who participate (if there are any) since they do it only on the basis of a sense of duty or habit, not because the program helps them in their own lives. But those programs also frustrate the people who lead them because a program that does not meet needs is not attended well.

Therefore, begin by observing the different types of people in your church and in your community. What does a typical church member look like? Does such a profile even exist? Or are there different subgroups in the church, e.g., an older "traditional church" expecting to be cared for and a "young church" that is searching for new forms of being the church? What is the age structure of the church? Social background? Are there single parent households? Young families? Who lives in the ministry radius of the church? Are you dealing with a mature neighborhood? Or is your church located in a new growth area?

Furthermore, ask about the needs of these groups of people within and outside the church. Better yet: ask the people themselves. Listen to them and observe where they hurt, what preoccupies them, how they spend their time, and what their life looks like. You should be able to list specific needs for each type of person.

Then consider which ministries could meet those needs. If you have a large group of singles, a ministry for singles could be right; or recreational activities that are not dominated by the needs of young families with children; or a retreat for singles; or a seminar evening focusing on the subject of "dealing with loneliness." For each need, specific activities or programs can be identified. Let your imagination run free. Deciding which of these ideas are actually practical for you to implement can be determined later. At that time you can also consider other factors like existing resources and the framework conditions of your church.

Exercise 33: Write down one or two ministry focus groups of your church. Identify at least three needs for each group and consider which kind of ministries could meet those needs. You can use our example of singles to get you started in your thoughts.

Ministry Focus Group	Needs	Ministry/Activity
Singles	Relationships	Singles Meeting, Seminar: Loneliness
	Continuing Education	Class for New Believers Cooking Class
	To Enjoy Life	Sports Retreat Concert
_____	_____	_____
_____	_____	_____
_____	_____	_____
_____	_____	_____
_____	_____	_____
_____	_____	_____
_____	_____	_____
_____	_____	_____

Step 2: Define success criteria that can be monitored.

Define Your Criteria of Success

What are the results you want to see as you offer a specific program? Here, we typically encounter two problems: First, we often have difficulties formulating measurable and visible criteria; second, we often state the wrong criteria.

If you want to monitor the success of your steps, you need to be able to observe and measure the results. For instance, count how many people participated in a program. Determine how many "decisions" have been made. Examine if a training program has yielded new workers for the church. Measure if the quality index of the church has grown. Criteria that meet these standards can also be stated as: "The concert was a success if thirty percent of those attending were non-Christians." Or: "The small group has met its goal when a) those attending express the subjective feeling 'I am getting something out of being part of this group!' and b) it multiplies itself within eighteen months." Or: "The children's ministry for the six to ten year-olds is successful when children come to faith on a regular basis, grow in faith and the parents comment enthusiastically about the group."

It is important in the context of natural church development that the criteria you define are based on biotic principles. A small group that defines group division as success respects the principle of multiplication. If parents comment that the children's ministry is "great" you can be sure it meets real needs and has not worked against the principle of energy transformation. A concert that aims at reaching a non-Christian audience pursues a worthy goal. But organizers interested in natural church development should think a step further. A concert is only a functional step for church growth when follow-up and integration of new believers into the local church is part of the overall vision.

Exercise 34: *Define some measurable and biotic criteria for all the programs listed in exercise 33.*

Ministry	Criterion	
_____	_____	_____
_____	_____	_____
_____	_____	_____
_____	_____	_____
_____	_____	_____
_____	_____	_____
_____	_____	_____
_____	_____	_____

Make Sure it Can Be Monitored

Step 3: Determine how you want to measure the results.

If in step 2 you have defined measurable criteria you probably have already thought about how you want to monitor them. As long as your criteria cannot be measured, they make no sense.

How do you find out if 30 percent of the concert attendees were non-Christians? Sometimes you will have to rely on estimates, but sometimes it is possible to prepare a program in such a way that more specific monitoring of results is possible. For instance, you could sell your tickets exclusively through the medium of personal relationships. There will be no publicity or posters. Only church members are informed of the event. Tickets are sold only as double- or multi-packets—one or more for non-Christian friends. In this way the defined success criterion influences even the way publicity is done. Of course no event can simply be planned around a set of success-monitoring devices. But with some purposeful imagination, meaningful programs can often be combined with appropriate monitoring mechanisms. Multi-usage!

Exercise 35: How can you concretely measure the criteria you have determined above? Are they indeed measurable?

Criterion	Kind of Measurement
_____	_____
_____	_____
_____	_____
_____	_____
_____	_____
_____	_____
_____	_____
_____	_____

Evaluate Results

Step 4: Evaluate the results.

After an event has taken place, you should apply your evaluation criteria. Ongoing programs are best monitored on a regular basis. At least once a year (and after any unusual event) you should list all your programs and ask: Which were successful? How successful were they? (Refer to your criteria!) Where did we see failures? Why?

Step 5: Have the courage to slaughter holy cows.

Slaughtering Holy Cows

Activities that were once meaningful do not stay that way indefinitely. Therefore, repeatedly evaluate with an open mind those types of programs which have been obviously successful. If tent-evangelism was successful in leading people to Christ ten years ago, does it still fulfill this purpose today? Even the most venerated programs need to be evaluated by the functionality criterion. Do not be afraid to critically evaluate even the "holy cows" if you truly care about church development.

Develop Functional Steps

Now we will again work through the three problems described on page 129. We have already worked on them in the last few chapters, but this time we will address them from the perspective of the principle of functionality. You will notice that this principle is very well suited to evaluate all the measures you have developed in the previous chapters.

Exercise 36: Read again through the two examples on page 129 then write down your answers to the questions on worksheet 3 (page 220); please make a copy for each of the examples. Then do the same exercise for the example from your church that you selected on page 129.

Work through each example according to the following points:

1. *Bring together all the steps and measures you have developed in the last five training chapters.*

2. *For each measure define a criterion for success that is in harmony with biotic principles.*

3. *Describe how you want to measure your criterion.*

This Is How You Could Have Proceeded

On the following page you will find our thoughts concerning some of the measures suggested in the previous training units in view of example 2.

Reflect on Your Ideas

Here we want to again evaluate the preceding exercise by reflecting on our own thought process. How did you find solutions to Exercise 36? What thought strategies did you use? How did you work over and improve your solution, maybe even after you read our suggested solution?

Exercise 37: Using Worksheet 3 (page 220) take at least fifteen minutes to reflect on your own thought process as you found solutions to Exercise 36.

Part 4: Learning to think biotically

Worksheet: Developing Functional Structures

Step:	Criterion:	Measurement:
Improve the coaching of workers	1 supervisor for every 3-4 workers	The ratio is a visible fact. Supervisors will keep track of the number of coaching appointments
Train apprentice counselors	Every counselor trains at least one apprentice counselor a year	By counting
Pastoral conversation with the minister	1. Trust relationship with the pastor 2. Perceived as helpful by the worker	1. Can be measured only subjectively 2. Ask for feedback
Find a new worker	New worker has been recruited, he has the following gifts …	Giftedness can be examined through the gift test
Train the small group	Small group participants exhibit more "social competence"	Success will become visible in future crisis situations
Worker leads out in a self-help group	Other couples are benefited by his ministry	Questionnaire among participants

Suggestions for Group Learning

Again remember the guidelines for group exercises already mentioned in the preceding chapters:

1. Before you conduct the exercises, group members should have a basic knowledge of functionality.

2. Use images, pictures, and stories when you explain the principle of functionality to your group members and watch for those "aha" effects.

3. Always begin with an easy exercise.

4. During each exercise, plan enough time for evaluation.

Introduction

In your own words summarize the first section of this chapter. Perhaps you could use the "story of the roast" and the "test question" to explain the meaning of functionality in the context of natural church development.

For the remaining exercises, decide up front if you want to work on evaluating existing programs, or if you want to generate new programs and activities using functional principles.

Present the appropriate steps from the sections "Evaluating Existing Programs" (page 176) or "Creating New Functional Programs" (page 179).

Instructions for exercises 30-32

If you have decided to evaluate existing programs you can proceed using Worksheet 9 (page 226). Discuss each of the following points in your group (form subgroups if you have more than five participants).

• Select a program, a measure, or an activity you want to evaluate according to the principle of functionality.

• Define a success criterion that is in harmony with biotic principles.

  Describe carefully how you will measure this criterion.

• Repeat this exercise with other examples.

Instructions to exercises 33-35

If you have decided to create new programs integrating the principle of functionality, you should orient yourself on a real live situation and not just do a theoretical exercise. As a group, select a program which is already in the planning stage and will be conducted in the near future. Then discuss each of the following points in your group (form subgroups if you have more than five participants).

• Which needs does this activity/program address? Is this measure really need-oriented?

- Define measurable success criteria for this activity that are in harmony with biotic principles.

- How can we measure these criteria concretely? Are they really measurable?

- Set a date for evaluating the results of this activity.

Instructions to exercise 36

You probably do not have the time to work through all the examples (our two and your church related one) as a group. First decide which examples you will actually work on. Then for the selected example, bring together all the results from the previous training units in one visible place for everyone (using a board or a flip chart). Next let every participant fill out Worksheet 8 for the selected example. The solutions found are discussed first in groups of three, and finally presented in the plenary group.

Instructions to exercise 37

Ask each participant to work individually through the questions of the worksheet. After fifteen minutes, ask participants to share their thoughts in groups of three. Each triad is asked to make a list of successful and unsuccessful thought strategies with which all participants can identify (even if they have not applied them themselves). The lists are then presented to the whole group.

Training Unit 7: Finding and Evaluating Solutions

If you have worked through all the previous training units you now have six partial solutions before you of different situations calling for a decision. The purpose of this unit is to arrive at a biotic comprehensive answer, that is a solution that integrates all six biotic principles at once. By now, this may come quite easily for you.

"It makes sense to develop solutions, first intuitively, and then evaluate them."

Perhaps you noticed that in the previous units many ideas and approaches to solutions repeated themselves or at least pointed in the same direction. That is because the biotic principles do not stand for independent rules or principles that compete with each other. In fact, they simply embody six different approaches to answer a single question: What can we do in our churches to reinforce those growth automatisms God uses to build His church?

From the Whole to the Part to the Whole

Until now, we have always started with a single biotic principle, a part of the whole. In reality, however, the process of developing a biotic solution proceeds in exactly the opposite direction. It is much simpler to first develop different alternative solutions intuitively, which are then examined for their biotic qualities only in a second step. This approach then allows you to integrate the best elements into a new solution. Thus the process of finding a biotic solution consists of four steps:

Step 1: Train biotic thinking.

Learning to Think Biotically

You have already started when you decided to work through the training program. Of course, it is a lifelong process to improve your grasp of the patterns of God's workings, and that is all biotic principles are trying to communicate, but it is a good beginning. If we compare the goal to be reached—to develop the church of Jesus Christ in harmony with God's principles of growth—with the North Pole, then you no longer need a sign at every street corner reading "Here is the direction to the North Pole." You have now acquired your own compass that can show you the right direction (even if this compass may be a bit imprecise in the beginning).

Step 2: Develop several alternative solutions intuitively.

Making Intuition Work for You

This step challenges you to think holistically. In the beginning as you look for biotic solutions and approaches, don't get bogged down with too many details (looking for direction signs). Just take your inner compass and look for several possibilities to reach your goal.

Don't insist on the first possibility suggested as the final solution. Rather adopt a relaxed brainstorm mode that is open for new and innovative ideas, possibly together with other leaders or workers. The biggest mistake in the attempt to find a solution is often collecting too few alternatives. If you find one (and only one) good solution, it could be that you are overlooking numerous better solutions. A good rule is to never be satisfied with less than three alternative possibilities.

Examining Alternatives

Step 3: Critically examine the alternatives.

In step 2, your perspective was focused on the whole. Now it is time to examine the particulars. The process depends on your experience in biotic thinking and the complexity of the problems that need a solution. The more you have been immersed in biotic principles the easier it will be for you to evaluate the list of alternatives intuitively without analytic processing. For "smaller" decisions, this step tends to get worked out more and more automatically. For more complex solutions, proceeding systematically is always the best strategy. For this reason we have included on worksheets 10 and 11 (pages 227-228) some checklists that are designed to test your alternative solutions in view of their capacity to liberate the potential that God has already put into your church.

Putting Together the Partial Answers

After focusing on the particulars, we must finally turn again to the whole. At this stage we are possibly aiming at a new creative process to filter all the good activity elements out of the different alternative solutions, then integrate them into a new solution. Normally, none of the original alternatives will emerge as the one perfect solution while all others are unusable. On the contrary, each solution often contains valuable aspects. Because you have examined in step 3 all alternatives with the help of the checklists (worksheets 10 and 11) you are now able to identify the most valuable elements. The checklists help you to find out which of the biotic principles have been observed or neglected.

As you look at all the alternatives, select the one that has emerged as the best one and try to improve it by integrating into its weak parts the best aspects of the other solutions. If your best solution applies all principles except "multiplication" you might be able to incorporate some ideas in view of this principle from other solutions. If even the remaining alternatives do not yield anything for this principle, you'll want to reexamine this solution again. It is best to do this systematically using the appropriate training chapter as a help in the process.

Your Personal Solution

Now it is time to turn theory into practice. Using the three examples that you have repeatedly worked with in the last few chapters, you should now practice how to arrive at a comprehensive biotic solution.

Exercise 38: Please work through each example using the following steps:

1. Using an intuitive approach, find several alternative solutions for each problem. You surely remember some of the partial solutions. Try now to find a comprehensive solution without looking up the previous ones. Write it down on a sheet of paper.

2. Examine the alternative solutions using the checklists (worksheets 10 and 11, pages 227-228) and assess to what degree your measures reflect biotic principles.

3. Now improve the best solution by incorporating aspects of other alternatives or reexamine the solution to make it more biotic. Reevaluate the new solution using the checklists.

Reflect on Your Ideas

As we conclude this training program we want to again evaluate the preceding exercise by reflecting on our own thought process. How did you find solutions to Exercise 38? What thought strategies did you use? How did you work over and improve your solution? Try to think again through the whole process of finding a biotic solution.

Exercise 39: Using Worksheet 3 (page 220) take at least fifteen minutes to reflect on your own thought process as you found solutions to Exercise 38. Did you notice that you are proceeding differently than at the beginning of the training program?

| Part 4: Learning to think biotically | # Suggestions for Group Learning |

After so many single exercises, you have earned a chance to finally develop a comprehensive solution with your group and celebrate the conclusion of this training program. But first some work:

Instructions to exercise 38

Divide the whole group into subgroups of three and work with them through the steps presented in exercise 38. You will notice that in the context of a group it is much easier to find several alternatives (especially if you are using brainstorm techniques). The examination of alternatives is also more thorough and exciting. Finally, each triad can present their solution to the plenary group and even at this stage improvements are possible.

Instructions to exercise 39

Ask each participant to work individually through the evaluation sheet. After fifteen minutes, ask them to share their thoughts in groups of three. Each triad is asked to make a list of successful and unsuccessful thought strategies with which all participants can identify (even if they have not applied them themselves). The lists are then presented to the whole group. In this round, pay special attention to the changes participants have experienced in their own thinking in the course of this training program.

Quiz

If you think that such a comprehensive task as exercise 38 is not the right kind of conclusion for this training program, or not in line with the celebration atmosphere at the end of such a process, you could conduct as your last exercise (or as an alternative) the following quiz.

Divide the participants into subgroups of three that will compete with each other. One of the groups begins with question 1 which is to be answered as quickly and intuitively as possible, observing biotic principles. (There is a time limit of two minutes per question before the turn goes to the next group.) The solution is then discussed with the other groups using the checklists. For each checklist question that is answered "biotically," the group gets one point. Notice that even "right" answers do not always earn the full number of points because the solutions are different in complexity and some of the checklist questions do not really apply to each solution. (Remember it is only a game!)

Then it is the next group's turn with question 2, etc. In the end the group that has collected the most points is appointed "chief consultant for natural church development."

Quiz

1. Your small group has grown to 15 participants. What do you do and how do you do it?

2. The worship service of your church suffers from meager atten dance. The church leaders wonder how to invite other people. What possibilities do you see?

3. Your church profile revealed that "loving relationships" is your minimum factor. What do you do with this result?

4. A church member indicates that he/she wants to get involved in the ministry of the church, but only under the condition that he/she finds a task that he/she can enjoy. How do you respond?

5. Some church members who read their Bible on a daily basis complain that the texts are sometimes difficult to understand and that they are not getting much out of it. Your reaction?

6. You intend to introduce in your church the concept of gift-oriented ministry. But you discover that for some tasks, there are no Christians with the appropriate gift. How do you deal with this?

7. During a church board meeting it is suggested to change some forms in the church—for instance the worship service and the evangelistic program—to make the church more attractive for visitors. What is your opinion?

8. Some workers insist that their responsibilities should be limited to a certain period. What do you do?

9. Over and over, members resign abruptly from their responsibilities because they are too stressed out. What would have to happen to decrease the frequency of these situations?

10. The children's ministry needs more workers. How can you win new ones?

11. The youth ministry hopes to hire a part-time staff member, but realizes that the financial resources are too limited. How could it be done anyway?

12. In your church, almost all the members have discovered their gifts with the help of the gift test. Yet none of the hoped-for, positive changes are taking place. What could have gone wrong and how could the situation be improved?

The Most Frequently Asked Questions About Natural Church Development

When Christians get involved in natural church development, similar questions come up again and again. In the following pages you will find the most frequently asked questions that come to us partly from correspondence, partly from our church growth seminars. Most answers are based on taped transcriptions of real Q & A situations.

Most Frequent Mistakes

What would you describe as the most frequent mistake of churches trying to work according to natural church development principles?

The most frequent mistake is probably to confuse *talking* about the principles of natural church development with *practicing* them; confusing the reading of a book with concrete steps for implementation; confusing the conducting of a church survey with working through its practical consequences. The principles of natural church development do not come alive because we talk about them in church committees or even in sermons. What is crucial is the extended, often difficult and even conflict-ridden process of putting them into practice—step by step.

Another frequent mistake consists of selectively picking out certain segments of natural church development, such as partial aspects of gift-oriented ministry or need-oriented evangelism, while at the same time ignoring that we are dealing here with a holistic system in which all the particular parts need to work together.

Third, we often observe that churches start to tackle the minimum factor with great diligence but work at it with a technocratic or spiritualizing arsenal of methods. In many cases, churches try to integrate certain techniques of natural church development into a theological framework that is not compatible with this approach.

Where is the Success?

Theoretically these principles certainly make sense. But where are the examples that the whole approach also works? Is it really true that all the churches that are working with this approach are also growing?

Your question can be answered from two perspectives. We could select all the growing churches and see to what degree they are applying the principles of natural church development. We can also proceed differently and take all the churches that obviously apply these principles and examine how consistently they are growing. Thanks to the research projects we conducted, both questions can be investigated quite precisely.

The most exciting discovery of our research project was that the majority of all quantitatively growing churches are working with the principles of natural church development. Thus, if you are looking for examples for this approach to church growth, look at the churches that are experiencing qualitative and quantitative growth. These are "models" for natural church development, even if they have not even heard the term yet. Natural church development is not merely an abstract theory which somebody invented at his desk. We are dealing with a practical approach which can be shown to be used by growing churches around the globe.

The second perspective proceeds, not from the growth of the church, but from the application of the principles. The question underlying this approach is, "Is such and such a church truly *applying* the principles?" The only objectively measurable criterion is the assessment of the quality index. By doing a church profile a second, third, or fourth time, a church can find out how effective it is in putting the principles into practice. Churches we have observed over longer periods of time and who have consistently applied the principles, have had good experiences with it. To support this statement, here are a few statistics: 84 percent of all churches that have done a church profile several times and have made measurable progress in view of their minimum factor have also experienced numerical growth. And without exception, wherever a quality index of 65 was reached in all eight areas—in other words, wherever the principles of natural church development have been applied in especially consistent ways—churches grow also quantitatively.

I could tell you exciting stories of churches that have worked according to these principles and experienced growth. But I am rather hesitant, because such examples do not prove anything. Many Christians are searching for instant recipes, much like some are using popular weight loss diets, and they are impressed by testimonials: "Before I used this powder I was overweight, then I used it, now I am slender. Thanks for your powder!" They forget that the crucial element is not the magic powder but a healthy lifestyle. Natural church development wants to offer not more and not less. Whoever confuses the use of the church profile with such a magic powder will be greatly disappointed.

Church growth is simply too complex a matter to be evaluated by asking the question: "Has this one measure caused the church to grow?" As a church develops, it goes through a multi-level process in which the shift from numerical stagnation to growth is only one of countless stages. To focus your attention exclusively on the question of whether a non-growing church breaks through to growth would be just as simplistic as looking at the process of conversion solely by focusing at the moment of surrender to Christ, but ignoring the important processes before and after.

All the collected empirical data confirms the thesis that any—even a small—quality improvement in the church can be seen as a real success. Whenever I do tell success stories, I often select churches whose quality index rose after many conflicts from "greatly below average" to just "below average," but who do not yet experience quantitative growth. I also include churches that have grown rapidly for years with only average quality, and who are now consciously turning their attention to the quality characteristics.

Overestimating Reflection

Is it true that growing churches are continuously dwelling on these principles?

No, but this is not the point. What matters is not how much or how little you are thinking about these principles, but only that they are put into practice. If that can be done successfully with a minimum level of reflection—I would almost say all the better.

The other day a pastor friend of mine told me: "Since we stopped applying the principles of natural church development, our church is growing numerically." Of course I wanted to know more about this so I said: "Why don't we take a look and see if what you say is really true. Let's take some of the eight basic principles, for instance "loving relationships" and "passionate spirituality." If I understand your words correctly you want to tell me that today there is less love expressed in your church than before, there is less prayer and less listening to the will of God." He interrupted me: "Of course I don't mean that," he said. "No, the relationships are more loving than before and the spiritual life has become more devoted." "Then this means that you are applying the principles today more consistently," I replied. "So it does not surprise me that your church is also growing numerically."

What this pastor meant was simply that instead of talking and thinking about the principles, today they concentrate on putting them into practice. A large portion of the ministry of our institute consists of critical reflection. But reflection is, at best, a subsidiary background ministry and very often not the strategic key to transformation.

Only a few people get involved in something new because they have been convinced on the basis of rational arguments and facts. Most people make their decisions because of emotional, non-rational motives. If in natural church development we forget to take this fact seriously, the best biblical arguments and the most exact research findings will not be able to help us.

Terms That Are Too Abstract

Your principles make sense to me, but we have a hard time with your terminology. Could the whole concept not be expressed in more popular language?

Yes, it should. I encourage churches to translate the terms in more pictorial language that fits their culture and spiritual tradition. Thus "passionate spirituality" has already become "joy in Jesus," "being filled with the Holy Spirit," and "full surrender to the Lord." This terminology fits at the level of preaching and counseling better than the abstract term "passionate spirituality." However, the popular terms that one church coins do not fit the situation of other churches. The work of interpretation and transfer must be done by each church. The less abstract a term, the better it communicates, but the narrower its capacity to serve as a symbol for the diversity of possible translations. When you deal with generally applicable principles it lies in the nature of things that terms become more abstract.

Is it really spiritual to want to analyze the growth of the church with statistical methods?

The main reason why many of us consider such an approach unspiritual and suspect seems to be that we are not familiar with these methods. Most people tend to judge anything foreign in a negative way, at least, at first contact. Non-Christians may react with the words, "I don't like that!" while Christians tend to react, "This is unspiritual!" I went through a similar experience in view of church surveys. My thinking changed at this point only when I saw the fruit of this work.

What do statistical methods help us with? Generally, they sharpen our perceptions for the normal, preventing us from mistaking exceptions for rules. Our research shows us how church growth happens "as a rule," while some of the literature on this subject tends to focus especially on exceptions. Both approaches are legitimate, but they do not have the same spiritual benefit. One big problem is that many Christians who identify themselves with spiritualizing thought patterns attach greater spiritual significance to the exceptions to the rule than to the rules themselves.

Let me illustrate with an example that does not come from the sphere of the church. Medical research has determined that smoking is harmful to your health and shortens your life expectancy. But you can point to contrary "evidence" and say: "But our uncle Joe smoked every day and reached the age of 94." Does your story disprove the statistical findings of medical research? No, the mentioned uncle Joe represents an exception to the rule. But here is the point: Which statement is more important, helpful, and relevant for people? That on the average smokers die earlier, or that uncle Joe reached 94 years of age? The first statement would encourage the realization: "We better be afraid of smoking," but the second statement would actually encourage the attitude: "Let us smoke happily!" This example shows how dangerous it would be to replace a statistical statement about what is normally right with a comment about some isolated experiences.

This applies also to the growth of the church. While there are exceptions—churches that grow without using the principles of natural church development—it would be devastating if we would make them our standard model. The statistical approach helps us to carefully distinguish between such isolated cases and generally relevant principles. Why some consider this approach more unspiritual than to spread church reports along the "uncle Joe" model, I do not understand.

Technocracy **You dispute the charge of technocracy, at the same time you use computers and work with statistical methods and mathematic formulas. Is this not very technocratic?**

No. While our approach is empirical it is in no way technocratic. Those two terms have nothing in common. In fact, natural church development endeavors to overcome technocratic thinking. But this cannot be done on the basis of feelings according to the motto: "This is wrong because I don't like it." We have to proceed on the basis of reliable proof. Therefore we had to use valid rational methods.

We have attempted to develop our argument on two levels: first, on the theological-foundational level, and second, with the tools of the empirical social sciences. A clear, logically valid and reliable test construct has basically nothing to do with technocracy. To generally exclude empirical methods is at best a symptom for spiritualizing thought patterns, but theologically speaking, it does not have any advantages over an empirical approach.

Objectivity **Are your research findings really objective? Does it not depend on the questions you use to approach the subject?**

You are right. The way you ask questions influences the research results considerably. This is also true for the presumably objective natural sciences. The ancient scientific ideal of the absolute certain knowledge (epistéme) has been shown to be an idol. Even the most direct perception has already been filtered, based on value judgments and interpretations.

Thus any scientific model highlights certain parts of the research object and leaves out other aspects. It illuminates a complex reality, shedding light on some segments, while leaving others in the dark. The chemical-physical method, for instance, recognizes only the chemical and physical aspects of living organisms and ignores other aspects. This is entirely legitimate and even helpful. In this way we get answers for certain questions while other questions, e.g., the philosophic, theological question of the nature of life, cannot be answered using this method.

This is also true for the church. I can look at this phenomenon from the most diverse perspectives. I can approach it with different methodologies, e.g., biblical-exegetical, church historical, or also with the help of the methodologies of the social sciences. Each of these perspectives answers certain questions but does not answer other questions. Our research answers the question: "What are the universally valid quality characteristics that have a positive relationship to the growth of Christian churches?" This question does indeed reflect our pre-research interest in the growth of churches. Is this unscientific? No, because scientific neutrality does not exist, there are only different interests which are then dealt with scientifically.

Some have commented critically that we are losing our objectivity by not limiting ourselves to the research study, but offering at the same time practical helps for the development of the church. Behind this objection hides the widespread thought that the exclusion of application questions is the best guarantee for objectivity. Let me make one thing very clear: We do not belong to the kind of scientists who do "pure" research, supposedly not contaminated by any "purpose," and who then pride themselves that they are staying out of questions of benefit and application. On the contrary, our research was designed expressly against the horizon of practical application. We do not consider this a disadvantage but a considerable advantage in contrast to "purely academic" discussions.

It is noteworthy that, in essence, the findings of the international study confirm what you have been teaching already for years. It seems therefore that your principles were already determined before hand, and that you may have designed the study in such a way that you got the desired results.

Favorite Ideas Confirmed

What you are saying is not entirely false. When we started the international study we did not have to start at point zero, thanks be to God! Instead we could build on what was already indicated in our previous studies. Even our first research study in German-speaking Europe did not start from scratch, but built on the then current knowledge level of church growth research. At every stage of our research studies, we later integrated new questions to find out if there are other principles that have a positive relationship with church growth. In this way we have learned many new things during the last ten years.

Our international study has confirmed most of what we or others had discovered earlier. But it also pointed out some weaknesses in our understanding, and even some things that were wrong. In any case, we learned so much through this international research project that we are now in the process of thoroughly revising all the practical books we have published before the study, in the light of the research findings.

How can you claim that the principles you discovered in the churches surveyed are also applicable to all other churches?

Universally Applicable

This is a stimulating question which church growth research shares with any empirical science. Take for instance the following scientific statement: "All copper is a conductor of electricity." If you were to verify this sentence experientially you would have to examine all copper in the universe in view of this quality, which of course is impossible. Thus the attempt to verify does not help us farther along, but the inverse approach does: We can try to disprove this theory, to falsify it. When can a theory be regarded as "true"? According to Karl Popper, when until now it has stood the test of all attempts to falsify it. However, according to Popper's theory of knowledge, a theory is not regarded as falsified when it is contradicted by some observations here and there. A theory is only considered falsified when it is succeeded by a better one.

What does this mean in view of our question? The 65-hypothesis, which says that any church which has reached a quality index of 65 or more in all eight quality characteristics is growing, has not been falsified by a single case. Suppose we find the first exception to the rule tomorrow, would that mean that the whole theory is false? Not at all. It would be false only if there would be a system that can explain the growth of churches in a more conclusive, helpful and reliable way than our explication based on the eight quality characteristics.

In order to establish generally applicable principles in the realm of the social sciences it is important that the surveyed sample is large enough. The selection of 1000 churches worldwide is more than adequate to come to general conclusions which are applicable to other churches. The samples for any single country, however, are usually not large enough to make conclusive statements about that subgroup. This is the reason why we refrain from making statements based on small national samples.

The Greatest Surprise

What surprised you most in your research?

That, on average, the smaller churches are the better churches. To say it in a simplified way: "The larger, the worse." This pattern is so significant that it is difficult to see why no one else has come across this pattern. Instead some authors even proceed from the opposite thesis, namely "The bigger, the better."

The fog over this question is linked to a rather awkward fact. As long as we used the current attendance figures as our standard measurement, no such correlation was recognizable. The negative correlation between growing church size and church quality and evangelistic potential showed up only when we used church attendance figures from five years before as our standard measure. At first sight this selection seems to be rather arbitrary, but if you look closer it makes sense.

To categorize a church as "growing" or "non-growing" has to do with its real growth pattern in the past. We don't really know if a church will grow in the future. There are indications that we just cannot presume that past growth guarantees growth in the future. In fact, many churches that are large today owe their growth to typical growth dynamics found in smaller churches. But many churches that were large five years ago have stopped growing or are declining today.

It is therefore misleading to use the current church size as a basis for assessing the effects of that size and speak about future growth potential. The only possibility to correlate a certain church size with future development is to look at the size of the church in the past and interpret the present as the future that has already arrived and which can therefore be examined. Without this mental model, which at first was difficult for me to grasp, we would not have come across many of our new discoveries.

In the light of the new research what has emerged as your own biggest error?

Biggest Error

The greatest change surfaced in the area of the quality factor we today call "empowering leadership." We formerly spoke of "goal-oriented leadership," and before that even of "goal-oriented pastor." The change in terminology reflects the new insights we gained for this quality factor. Some of the things I said in the past about this subject I had taken too uncritically from other church growth authors. Many of them based their observations of leadership on leaders in large churches rather than growing ones. It can be demonstrated that large ones are characterized by completely different leadership styles than smaller ones. Thus if we do not follow the contrast "small versus large" but "growing versus non-growing" we encounter different principles. This is one of the reasons why I consider the attempt to develop church growth principles mainly on the basis of large churches as ambivalent.

How did the list of questions come into being that you used to develop the quality index for the different quality characteristics?

The Genesis of the List of Questions

The list of questions we used to conduct our first church growth surveys in 1987 resulted mainly from studying the church growth literature available at that time. In designing the first questionnaire, I tried to make use of those aspects that were common to most of the books. The result of this first research study at that time was the description of seven quality characteristics.

With each level of research, the questions changed as well as the association of the questions with certain quality characteristics. Each question which we have included in the analysis (the current questionnaire also contains a few items that play no role in the calculation of the quality index) have to meet two criteria: first, they must have a positive relationship to quantitative growth (criterion validity); second, they have to fit with the other items that a certain quality characteristic is based on (item analysis).

Today the linking of questions to a certain quality characteristic is done by the computer. This means that the survey questions are not associated with a certain quality factor because we believe it fits there best, but because there is a statistically significant correlation. Let me illustrate. One of 170 items on which the calculation of the quality index is based reads: "Our pastor involves many members in the development of the worship service." We formulated this sentence originally for the quality characteristic "inspiring worship service." But when we processed all 1000 churches, we realized that while a positive answer to this question correlated strongly with growth, there was practically no statistical relationship to the quality factor "inspiring worship service." Instead we noticed that this question had a lot to do with "empowering leadership" and is now associated with this characteristic. Similar comments could be made about many questions which have gone through changes in the last ten years.

Biblical Principles Are More Important

Who determines what should be termed "quality" in a church? Biblical criteria are much more important than your quality characteristics which were identified by empirical studies.

I can tell you how we went about developing our "quality index." We proceeded on the basis of the then unproved axiom that *everything that has a positive relationship with the quantitative growth of a church—is "quality."* Thus our point of departure for analyzing quality was at first a quantitative one. But notice we started with growth—not church size. We did not do this because we felt the quantitative criterion was the most intelligent, inasmuch as research has now demonstrated that the question for quality yields much stronger evidence. But we did not know that until after we had finished the research study, not before we started. What we needed in the beginning was an external criterion which could be determined in a fairly objective way. In a similar way, researchers use school grades as an external criterion when they develop the intelligence quotient. In this way, we avoided the trap of defining what church quality is on the basis of our understanding of the Bible, only to exclaim triumphantly: "Look, these churches have superior quality" once we found those indicators in some of the churches.

In a second step, we critically examined all the emerging principles by biblical standards. To say it in an exaggerated way: The research could have shown that in growing churches people drink more Coca-Cola and that their pastors wear blue shoes, or (more realistically) leaders use more manipulative means than in non-growing churches. Suppose research had led to such conclusions, how would we have dealt with them? Well, at first we would have taken notice of these interesting findings. We might even have published some of them. But we would not have integrated these insights into our practical instructions for other churches because none of these three observations could have been maintained in the light of biblical examination.

But such considerations are, of course, purely hypothetical, since all the factors which have been shown to have a positive relationship with church growth are in harmony with the overall teachings of the Bible. Thus at least the foundational principles of natural church development—the eight quality characteristics—can rightly be called "biblical principles." In short: Biblical statements were not the starting point for our research. Rather, they served as a critical standard against which we examined what we found empirically.

You intentionally seem to adopt a theologically neutral stance, but when one takes a closer look at your positions they reveal a theology that is evangelical. Without a personal relationship to Jesus your model would simply not hold together.

Our starting point is the question: "What are the reasons some churches grow, and others do not?" This is first of all a question which has nothing to do with the theological convictions of those who conducted the research. When it comes to our conclusions, you can call some of the results evangelical, especially in the area of "passionate spirituality," or "need-oriented evangelism." That would be your interpretation. But any church, no matter how evangelical it is or not, will have to deal with the *fact* that these are the principles that are relevant for any church interested in winning new people. If someone says defiantly: "I don't want that because this is too evangelical for me" he or she is really saying: "I don't want to win new people." Thus I find it extremely fascinating to discuss this thesis with representatives of different theological camps.

Are there any additional growth factors beyond the eight quality factors you describe?

Yes. There are "contextual factors" that can have a furthering or hindering impact on the growth of a church. Since we usually are not able to influence these external factors, they do not play a great role in our strategic considerations. We want to concentrate on those factors which can be influenced, and those are the eight quality characteristics.

From time to time I am asked if it is not possible that a ninth or tenth quality characteristic will be discovered in the future. Of course this is a possibility. But until now we have not really discovered factors that are positively related to the growth of the church which could not be subordinated to any of the eight quality characteristics.

Finally, there are a host of aspects which could truly be termed "church growth factors" in a given local church, such as "high quality organ music," or "seeker services," or certain forms of evangelism. But none of these factors are generally applicable principles. In natural church development we concentrate only on those growth factors which have been proven to be universally valid.

What you call church growth principles you have simply copied from secular management books and applied to churches.

Suppose your statement were true. Would this then discredit the principles? Only those which contradict biblical criteria. Some of the

Evangelical Theology

Other Growth Factors

Secular Principles

management principles accepted today fall into this category, e.g. principles that are based on a naïve glorification of capitalism or questionable views of human nature. But there are other principles of management that pass the test of spiritual examination. I believe that there is nothing objectionable in the process of studying secular management books and determining what could be transferred to the realm of the church and what could not.

But this was not my starting point. I discovered the principles through studying Christian churches. It was only after I had done that, that I noticed parallels to certain aspects of the current management literature. That I grew in my own understanding in this sequence was purely accidental. It could have been the other way around. But the spiritual validity of principles would not be affected in either case.

Representative Sample of Churches?

Are your studies really representative? Does this not depend totally on the kind of church you have studied?

No study can claim to be representative in a general way. The question is always, "Representative in what way?" In other words, which question does this study answer representatively? Our study is representative for answering the question of universally valid growth criteria of Christian churches. It is not representative for countless other questions, e.g. the question of the spiritual quality of Christianity worldwide, or the church growth potential of churches in a certain country, or the structural quality of non-charismatic Baptist churches in Flemish-speaking Belgium.

The diversity of studied churches (representing some 20 denominations in addition to many independent churches) is sufficient to ensure that the question our research tries to answer is dealt with adequately. If we were to eliminate 10 denominations from the analysis the results would change only slightly. By contrast if we were to add another 20 denominations the results would not be modified significantly. In publishing the results, we have limited ourselves to those that can be considered as representative for growing churches (and high quality churches).

Learning From Germany?

You've said Germany must be considered a spiritually underdeveloped country, not a model for others. Is it not then questionable to export a German model to other countries?

Yes, indeed. But natural church development is not a German model. It is based on principles God uses on all five continents to build his church. It explains the growth of churches in Russia as well as in Brazil, in the United States, in Germany or Korea. It is true that many popular church growth concepts contain countless culturally dependent characteristics true only for the model church in question along with a few generally valid principles. This is a mistake we do not want to make.

You claim that your eight quality characteristics are universally valid. But surely they are also conditioned by culture and time. I question if 200 years ago you would have had the same results. **Culturally Conditioned Results**

I can only speak for our time today since churches that existed 200 years ago can no longer be studied empirically. Moreover, the literature of that period has recorded only how these churches saw themselves, but no growth principles determined by actual research. Since we know today that there can be a great difference between literary self-perception and empirical research results, we may safely assume that this also applies to the past.

If we limit ourselves to speak for the present we can say this: The principles on which natural church development builds are demonstrably valid from Alaska to Vladivostok, from Greenland to the Falkland Islands, from the North Cape to the Cape of Good Hope. In other words: They are cross-culturally valid. The way these generally valid principles are put into practice, however, differs widely from one culture to the next. And that is a very good thing.

You talk a lot about "growing" and "non-growing" churches. But it could also happen that a church has given away many members to help birth new churches. In your statistics such a church might end up being categorized as "stagnant" or "declining" even though it has done exactly what should be done according to the will of God. **Definition of Growth**

To avoid such a judgment we have developed a relatively complex formula for growth which takes into account any members that have been released to be part of a church planting project. A church that had a worship attendance of 200 five years ago, but today has only 180 worshipers due to the fact it sent out 40, then 20, and another time 60 people, it is counted as a growing church.

On the one hand you say that the statistical probability of a church growing when achieving a quality index of 65 or higher is 99.4 percent. On the other hand you say that among the 1000 churches studied you have not yet found a single exception. How do these two statements go together? **The "65 Hypothesis"**

In statistics we can deal only with probabilities that already have a built-in allowance for error in view of the exactness of the survey. The statistical results mentioned therefore tell us: There is a probability that about every two hundredth church that has reached a quality index of 65 in all eight areas might not be growing. That it is statistically probable, however, does not mean that it is actually that way. It could be that we will collect the data of 500 churches that fit the 65 hypothesis without ever finding a single exception to this rule. That we have not yet found an exception also reflects the fact that among the 1000 churches studied the number of churches that fit the 65 hypothesis was clearly less than 200.

Why Only 30 Questionnaires?

Would the results of the church profile not be more exact if the questionnaire was filled out by all church members, and not only by the 30 people you suggested?

No. The results would even be less exact. This is because the questionnaire was not developed for a survey of all members. The selection of 30 members that the pastors consider to be part of the very center of the church is based on the assumption that the measurable quality in this circle allows significant conclusions as to the growth potential of the whole church. This assumption has been confirmed by the research. The questionnaire contains a number of questions that do not communicate beyond that "hard core." Furthermore, the results are comparable among churches only if all used 30 questionnaires.

Circular Reasoning

In most of the graphical illustrations in the book *Natural Church Development,* you show that churches with high quality achieve a better result in view of certain test items than churches with lower quality. But the test questions are the same questions you used to determine the quality index of a church in the first place. Are you not guilty of circular reasoning according to the motto "high quality churches have a high quality"?

This is exactly one of those traps which needs to be addressed by a clean test construction. This procedure is called "part-whole-correction." In our case it worked like this: To determine the relationship a certain item has with the quality index of the church (there are a total of 170 items) the item under discussion is not included in calculating the quality index. Since it is only one of 170 items that flows into the quality index there is practically no great difference, but this process ensures that there is no circular reasoning that is taking place.

Confusing Graphs

I have difficulties grasping the meaning of most graphs where you depict the research results through your matrix of four. For instance, it is not clear to me what the four percentages in each of the graphics are related to.

It is true that this type of graph does not communicate at first sight, but only when you have familiarized yourself with the categories of churches that are represented by these graphs. Then, however, these graphs are quite powerful.

Bear in mind that the positive relationship to growth as well as to quality, (which each of the items depicted in the graph have) cannot be proven through these kinds of diagrams, but only through a correlation coefficient. But this coefficient is so abstract that it can hardly be expressed in graphic form. And as a mere mathematical value it just does not communicate to most people. For this reason we had to look for a graphic form that was capable of illustrating the essential aspects of what natural church development is all about. We could not limit ourselves to two-dimensional perspectives ("In grow-

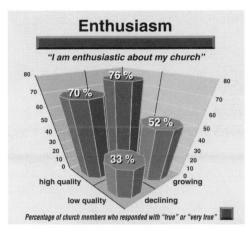

Enthusiasm

"I am enthusiastic about my church"

76 %
70 %
52 %
33 %

high quality
low quality
growing
declining

Percentage of church members who responded with "true" or "very true"

ing churches we found this, in non-growing churches we found that!"), but needed a graphic vehicle that would communicate the third dimension—church quality. Thus to illustrate the significance of each item, we selected four extreme groups: 1. churches with high quality that also grow quantita-tively; 2. churches with high quality that are at the same time declining (a rare phenomenon); 3. churches with low quality that grow quantitatively; and 4. churches with low quality that are declining.

Once you have selected the churches that fit into one of these four double-criterion categories, you can depict the percentage of members that answered a given question positively and whose church belonged to one of these four categories for each item.

Take a look at the graph in the upper left corner of this page. You see here the four categories of churches selected: in the front you have churches with low quality that are declining, in the farthest back you have high quality churches that are growing, on the right you have growing churches with low quality, on the left you find high quality churches that are declining. The height of the column indicates the percentage of members of a certain church category that either agreed "strongly" or "very strongly" with the statement above the graph: "I am enthusiastic about my church." In our example you see that 76 percent of the members belonging to growing churches with high quality agreed strongly or very strongly with this statement. In declining churches with low quality the percentage reached only 33, etc. But please note: We are not showing the answers of *churches,* as some have mistakenly assumed and which leads to confusion about the numbers. We are rather indicating the answers of individual *members,* and they usually answer quite differently, even when they belong to the same local church.

That the graphs are rather complex is caused by the fact that they must represent three dimensions in one graph type: church quality, quantitative growth, and the answer results of a certain question. If someone knows a better way to illustrate these contents, I would appreciate any suggestion. Until now I have not really found a clear alternative. What would not be helpful is to reduce the content matter of a three-dimensional character, for simplicity's sake, to a two-dimensional view. The biotic model cannot be displayed in just two dimensions. It is not by accident that the technocratic model tends to prefer two-dimensional illustrations, while the spiritualizing model is at war with any such computer generated graphs.

4.2 Million Answers

Could you give some details of how you ended up with 4.2 million answers during the research study?

A total of 1188 churches participated in this study with 34,314 persons filling out a questionnaire (the instructions asked for 30 church members and one pastor). In some cases we received less than 30 questionnaires, in some cases a few more. The questionnaire for pastors contained 108 items, the questionnaire for members and leaders had 91. This resulted in 3.1 million different answers. In addition, there were 194 churches that conducted the church profile repeatedly, and questionnaires from 238 churches that contained incomplete or incorrect data. Both of these groups could not be included in the analysis of the results according to churches. However, many of the single answers could be included in selected analysis, all in all, an additional 1.1 million answers.

The Most Important Quality Characteristic

You give the impression that all eight quality characteristics are equally important. But that is obviously misleading. Spirituality and especially prayer is certainly the most important.

I consider it counter-productive and not helpful—and biblically not justified—to work with a static list of predetermined importance according to the motto, "Prayer is more important than love, and both together are more important than worship but less important that evangelism, or vice versa." I have had the experience that almost all Christians tends to pick one of the eight quality characteristics and declare it "the most important" with great pathos.

If we agree that each church needs all eight quality characteristics, and if we furthermore agree that the existing minimum factor blocks the growth of a given church the most, we can approach the question, "Which factor is now the most important quality characteristic?" in a new light. Because the answer will probably differ considerably from church to church. What does "most important" mean if we cannot abandon any of the factors? All are vitally important and necessary. Is vitamin B more important for our bodies than vitamin C? There may be people who somehow conclude vitamin C is more important than vitamin B. But if someone suffers from a vitamin B deficiency an additional dose of vitamin C just won't help. In short: In different churches and at different times, the different quality characteristics can become "most important." We should beware of projecting our experiences on others.

On the one hand, you seem to argue strongly against a quantitative approach to church growth, but on the other you yourself are using one. The eight quality characteristics are based on the question: What do growing churches do differently? Thus you are proceeding from a quantitative criterion.

Quantity is Bad?

That we proceeded in our research from a quantitative criterion, namely the numerical growth of the church, is correct. But after proceeding from this quantitative criterion we identified the eight quality characteristics and learned that these characteristics are a much more helpful tool for church development. For this reason we are now using a qualitative approach. When you look at the potential for future quantitative growth there are many indicators for the following assumption: A church that is stagnating today, but has a high quality, will grow in the future with a greater probability than a church that is growing today but has a low quality.

My words reveal that I am fundamentally interested in the quantitative aspect of the church. What does quantity mean? In our context, it means people who are newly won to Jesus and the church. Anybody who can speak scornfully about quantity has not understood that behind each number is a person who is loved infinitely by God and who will spend eternity with him if he or she will respond to this love personally.

Therefore, our goal has never been to belittle quantitative growth. I simply consider it counterproductive to declare quantitative growth numbers the strategic goal of church development. That sort of growth is exactly that which we human beings cannot "produce," and it does not make sense to designate that which we cannot produce as the goal to be reached. If, however, we make the improvement of the quality of the church our goal, not based on some nebulous desire, but aiming at the improvement of the quality index in all eight areas and especially in view of the minimum factor, then we are focusing on something humans can influence. Research shows that if we concentrate with all our strength on this area, we can leave the question of quantitative growth to God. This statement should not be misunderstood as a cheap excuse for lack of growth. It simply is a theological interpretation of data we have collected during our research project.

You maintain that churches whose quality index lies below 50 are below average and churches above 50 are above average. When all the scores surpass 65 would you say that one can speak of revival?

Revival and the 65 Hypothesis

I would see it that way. In my opinion, this may be the most precise and at the same time most helpful definition of revival that I have encountered.

**Decline Despite
High Quality**

How do you explain that even high quality churches sometimes decline? According to your theory that should not happen.

Well, in "our theory" everything can happen that exists in reality. Remember we did not create a theory to which we adjust reality, but our theory is based on the observation of reality and changes as we make new discoveries. In the realm of empirical reality, we have indeed found churches that have above-average quality, but are declining. This applies to only 2 percent of all the churches we have studied and it is thus a very rare exception to the rule.

How can these exceptions be explained? In principle there are many possible reasons. It could be that certain unfavorable contextual factors become highly influential (e.g. people leaving the area because of unemployment problems). There could be inner-church factors that are not captured by the computer analysis, but which still block growth (e.g. lack of space). It is also conceivable that the church lost people due to members transferring to a newly planted neighboring church which uses a different style of spirituality that many members find attractive (this is possible also in high quality churches). Finally, it could simply be that the church has reached a growth ceiling and that God does not expect this church to continue to grow. Could it be an indication that this church should think more strongly about multiplication?

But even when we look at these very rare exceptions to the rule—they are all cases which at first sight seem to contradict the qualitative approach—we would never suggest that the problem could be really solved by now paying less attention to quality: from now on there will be less praying, less loving, less witnessing, etc. Perhaps there are other things besides working on the eight quality characteristics that need to be done in these cases, but never by abandoning church quality.

**Growth with Low
Quality**

How do you explain that, evidently, many churches experience growth which, according to your research, have a low quality?

This is another phenomenon that, in my experience, can be explained most often by contextual factors. A frequent constellation is the following: There is a gifted pastor who attracts a worship audience from a large region that features few attractive churches in the neighborhood. The people attend the worship service, listen to the sermon, go home, and return the next week—and that covers most of the "church life." Such a church might show up statistically as a growing church (based on increasing worship attendance figures), while seven out of eight quality characteristics might be hardly in existence. This is another illustration for the fact that the quality index is a stronger evidence than the purely quantitative growth experience of the church.

In this category we also encounter a different kind of problem. Some churches (we were able to study this phenomenon in Latin America) grow so rapidly that they are not able to catch up with the qualitative work. In these cases, the low quality index reveals a real problem which sooner or later tends to turn into a quantitative growth problem.

I can understand that you oppose the equation often found in church growth literature "large = good." But by reversing this conclusion into "large — bad" you seem to simply go too far.

Large equals bad?

With growth in size, the quality of the church as well as its evangelistic potential *decreases.* On the average, the generalizing equation is therefore correct that the larger the church, the worse it is. Of course, such average values never do justice to each single case. I know a great number of large churches—some of them included in our research—which reflect a high quality despite their large size. This is all the more remarkable because it is much more difficult in large churches to attain high quality than in smaller ones.

However, I am opposed to two things. First, the thought that every church should set the goal that it must become large. This unspoken (or sometimes explicit) orientation seems to me to be one of the greatest weaknesses of the church growth literature to this day. Second, I criticize the fact that principles of church growth are primarily deducted from observing large churches. But large churches are governed by different rules than smaller ones.

Large, high quality churches that are also growing are exceptions to the rule. I am convinced that in some cases God calls people to attempt such exceptions. As long as we do not make these churches the model for others, do not object. There are indeed some pastors who sense a clear call of God to lead such a large church. They also experience how this call becomes more and more reality. If we realize that this is a highly individual and extremely rare calling, we have all the more reason to rejoice in it.

In your opinion, what is the reason that most churches decrease in quality as they increase in size?

Reasons for Declining Quality

The most important reason seems to be that unlimited growth is non-biotic. Many approaches that advocate unlimited growth are much more based on the principle of *addition* than the principle of *multiplication.* If you look at the few megachurches that combine high quality with continuous growth you notice that they are almost always characterized by a "meta-structure." In other words, they are consistently structured into self-supporting subsystems—small, high quality churches if you like.

Many years ago, church growth research identified the phenomenon of growth barriers. Experience showed that at different sizes, growth seemed to stop without obvious reasons. The classic example is a church hitting a growth barrier when its worship attendance reaches

180-200. Today there are many resources dealing with the subject of "How to Break the 200 Barrier." Behind these resources often lies the unspoken assumption that it is a deficit when quantitative growth stops. But could it be that in many cases these growth barriers are actually "grace barriers"? Maybe God wants to tell us: "It is not good that your church is growing indefinitely. Instead of asking how to overcome these growth barriers, you should rather ask yourself how you can apply the principle of multiplication."

One thing is sure: Ten churches with one hundred worshipers each are sixteen times more effective evangelistically than a megachurch with a worship attendance of one thousand. And this despite (or maybe even because of) the fact that in small churches many things are done with much less "professionalism" than in large churches. Professionalism should never be confused with "quality" in the sense of the eight quality characteristics.

Fight Against the Church Growth Movement

In your material, one sometimes does not know if you intend to attack the church growth movement or if you consider yourself a part of it.

In no way do I view our work as an alternative to the church growth movement. The ministry of our institute is based on the foundational insights of personalities like Donald McGavran, C. Peter Wagner, Win Arn, and others. I myself have learned a great deal from them. They gave me the strong compulsion for the work I do today. And many of them have passionately supported us in view of our research project.

However, I am convinced that we cannot stop where we were. I believe that we need a new paradigm, in the church growth movement and in Christianity itself, to face the challenges of the future. When someone is committed to a new paradigm it does not mean that all the preceding work has been wrong. The building blocks that the church growth movement have furnished us with still retain their validity in the new paradigm. What the new paradigm offers is only a new framework of interpretation. It deals with the same set of data as before, but the data are integrated into a new system of mutual relationships. Try to look at certain statements, such as "church growth can be produced," through the eyes of a technocrat, a spiritualist, and a person who is used to thinking along the biotic categories of natural church development and you will understand what I mean.

Practice Instead of Mere Theory

You deal critically with model churches. But we have been greatly blessed by orienting our work towards a successful model church. What I like especially is that here we proceed from practice and not from theory, as natural church development does.

Objection! This is definitely not the heading that fits natural church development, because we insisted on *not* proceeding from theory but from practical reality. The object of our research project was pure practice, reality not invented in our own heads, not even in the minds of successful pastors (which is sometimes confused with reality), but rather practical reality as it can be identified on the basis of growing churches around the globe. We have consistently learned our principles from—in your words—"model churches." But notice carefully, not from one single model church, but from hundreds of very different types. The difference between principle- and model-oriented approaches is not one of theory versus practice, but between the practice of one single successful church and the practice of a great diversity of successful churches. We consider natural church development as "theory between practice and practice," to use a phrase from Helmut Gollwitzer. It originated in practical reality and it intends to transform reality. But between these two links to practical reality there is theoretical reflection.

When you get in touch with our resources—seminars, church profiles, workbooks—you will find that they contain, of course, the "theory," a theory that is based on practice and that wants to impact practice, but it is still theory. Now even though it can be quite helpful to deal with this theory, it is usually not the only motor for practical change. In fact, the personal encounter with a model church can sometimes work miracles. For this reason I can only highly recommend that one look at other churches thoroughly. However, if you are really concerned about a lasting transformation of your own church, you cannot limit yourself to just imitating the admired model church. Instead, you need to ask on your part: What are the aspects we want to transfer, which aspects do we want to modify, and which should we perhaps leave out? In other words, you yourself will be shifting from a model-oriented approach to a principle-oriented one. You cannot escape this process. And this "shifting" requires theoretical reflection.

Since you are admitting how helpful model churches are, why don't you utilize more of their concepts?

Models or Principles?

We use a principle-oriented approach in our own ministry for three reasons. First, we know that the principles that originate in this way have universal validity. Second, we know that these principles have a positive relationship to the growth of the church. And third, we know that these principles can be transferred into the most varying church situations. Despite all of the positive you can say about a model-oriented approach, these three points cannot be said about that which any single model church has to offer.

The Most Frequent Criticism

Which are the most frequent criticisms of your publications dealing with natural church development that you hear about?

Almost all critical voices can be assigned to one of three categories:

1. Most critics do not object to any statements they find in the books, but criticize what they *do not* find in a certain book. More than 90 percent of all critical remarks I have read in book reviews belong to this category. For instance, some have found fault with the fact that in *Natural Church Development* I do not deal sufficiently with the biblical theological foundations of the biotic approach, that the scientific methodology of our research project is not described sufficiently, or that it falls short on practical application for the local church. These critics are almost always right. It is true that every book does not deal with everything that could be said about a subject. Quite often the missing aspects of one book are dealt with thoroughly in another building block of natural church development. Our working materials have been developed as an organic system, and each book is just a building module. If every module dealt with everything, it would cease to be a system. On the other hand, if each building block would not integrate a holistic perspective at least seminally, the system would no longer be organic.

2. The second category of criticism has to do with different paradigms which communicate only with great difficulties with one another. Over and over again I hear that natural church development is nothing but a fairly "technocratic program." Others complain that the biotic approach is a hazy renunciation of strategic, programmatic and goal-oriented work. If we look at natural church development through the eyes of a "spiritualizer" or a "technocrat," these contrasting evaluations actually make sense.

3. The third category is of a very different nature. It consists of critical voices from people who are engaged in natural church development, and in the process are encountering certain problems which lead them to suggest improvements, corrections, and revisions. This is the source of criticism from which we ourselves learn the most. Indeed I would say that, besides the biblical texts and the empirical research it is the most important source that informs our working materials.

Paradigm Change

I consider your practical suggestions quite helpful. But it is not helpful that you combine them with fundamental theological positions as you do in the part dealing with the new paradigm. This just alienates many people unnecessarily.

I admit that these statements may alienate some readers, but I do not believe that this is something unnecessary. After all, the foremost barriers for church development do not exist on the level of lacking know-how, but at the level of deeply-rooted theological blockades. I am convinced that without a paradigm shift, our talk about church growth remains mere cosmetics.

As long as someone thinks, feels, and lives in technocratic or spiritualizing categories I might be able to win him or her for an activity or two if I succeed to persuade them, but I will never lead them to a passionate commitment to natural church development. Paradigm shifts are practically never the result of "carrot and stick" tactics. In short: Without provocation, without emotional excitement, without crisis—there simply is no paradigm shift.

I know quite well that we are now walking on thin ice. All the reading I have done on the subject of how to win others to a paradigm shift does not really convince me. I find that one of the most helpful and profound insights come from the physicist Max Planck, who said about these patterns of change: "A new scientific truth usually does not find acceptance because its opponents have been persuaded and admit that they have been convinced, but because the opponents gradually die out and the new generation that grows up is familiarized with the truth from the very start."

I fear that Planck is right with these words. When it comes to the recruitment of multipliers for church development, let us not concentrate on those who think in completely different paradigms. Instead, let us start with those who have already started to think in the dimensions of the new paradigm. And when I look at the world with these eyes, both at the local church level and internationally, I suddenly realize: "Man, there are not just a few of them."

Worksheet Masters for Copying

In this section you will find different worksheets which can assist you in your efforts for church development. Use these as your copy originals so you can use them repeatedly. By enlarging the copies 120 percent you will end up with a standard 8 1/2 by 11 inch format.

Worksheet 1
(Instructions on pages 108/109)

Worksheet: My Extended Family

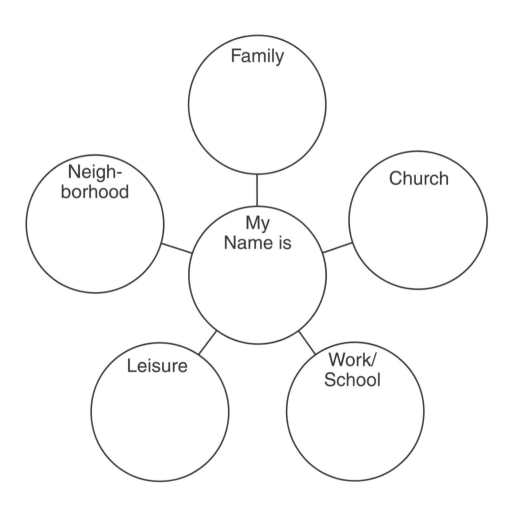

Worksheet: Develop a Network of Steps

Worksheet 2
(Instructions on
pages 129-132)

Problem: _____

_____

Area concerned:	short-term	long-term
Leadership	_____	_____
	_____	_____
Ministry	_____	_____
	_____	_____
Spirituality	_____	_____
	_____	_____
Structures	_____	_____
	_____	_____
Worship service	_____	_____
	_____	_____
Small groups	_____	_____
	_____	_____
Evangelism	_____	_____
	_____	_____
Relationships	_____	_____
	_____	_____

Worksheet 3
(Instructions on page 130)

Worksheet: Reflect about Your Thought Process

Take at least fifteen minutes to reflect about your thinking approach to the solutions for the different exercises.

This is how I approached the problem:

_____

_____

_____

_____

_____

_____

This was especially successful:

_____

_____

_____

_____

_____

_____

This led us nowhere:

_____

_____

_____

_____

_____

_____

Worksheet: Developing Multiplication Measures

Worksheet 4
(Instructions on
pages 143/144)

What aspects of multiplication could contribute to a solution for this situation? Develop concrete suggestions under the headings of "growth potential," "long-term effect," and "extending the production capacity"

_____

_____

_____

_____

_____

_____

Reevaluate your proposals carefully:

• *What would an addition solution look like? Has your solution a greater potential for growth?*

_____

_____

_____

_____

• *Is the long-term effectiveness of your solution greater (even if it takes longer in the beginning)?*

_____

_____

_____

• *What in this example is "production"? What is "the production capacity" here? Does this solution really increase the latter?*

_____

_____

_____

**Worksheet 5
(Instructions on
page 151)**

Worksheet: Energy Transformation

Step	Possible resistance:	Energy transformation:
_____	_____	_____
_____	_____	_____
_____	_____	_____
_____	_____	_____
_____	_____	_____
_____	_____	_____
_____	_____	_____
_____	_____	_____
_____	_____	_____
_____	_____	_____
_____	_____	_____
_____	_____	_____
_____	_____	_____
_____	_____	_____

Worksheet: Multi-Usage

Worksheet 6
(Instructions on
pages 162-164)

For each example work through all four steps consecutively using the following four questions:

- Step 1: What is the starting point? What is the intended goal?

_____

_____

_____

_____

- Step 2: What is the starting point here? What is the intended goal here?

_____

_____

_____

_____

- Step 3: How could step 2 be implemented?

_____

_____

_____

_____

- Step 4: How can step 1 be realized in dependence of the solution found in step 2?

_____

_____

_____

_____

Worksheet 7
(Instructions on
pages 170/171)

Worksheet: Symbiosis

Go through each example by working through each of the following points:

- When you look at the solutions to this example in the previous chapters, do you discover anywhere a tendency towards uniformity in your own solution?

_____

_____

_____

- Independent of your solution, what could uniformity look like in this context? How could it be avoided?

_____

_____

_____

- Is there any danger present in any of your solution attempts that might further competitive thinking? Where?

_____

_____

_____

- Independent of your solution, what could competitive thinking look like in this context? How could it be avoided?

_____

_____

_____

- Which symbiotic elements could be integrated into the solution?

_____

_____

_____

Worksheet:
The Tohuwabohu-Game

Worksheet 8
(Instructions on
page 173)

This game gives you a chance to get to know others and observe their behavior. The following list contains different skills and talents. Look for participants with these characteristics. Ask them about it and—if they have one let them sign on the appropriate line of the concerned quality.

Goal: to collect as many signatures as possible in the next ten minutes.

Signature:	**Quality:**
_____	I am very adaptive to life in another culture.
_____	I enjoy talking with non-Christians about Christ.
_____	I enjoy spending an hour or more praying.
_____	I have a positive outlook on life even when I encounter uncomfortable circumstances.
_____	It is not difficult for me to recognize wrong motives even behind spiritual sounding words.
_____	I plan my day and leave as little as possible to chance.
_____	I like to help people in very practical ways who are in trouble.
_____	It is easy for me to apply theoretical knowledge to concrete situations.
_____	I love to invite guests over.
_____	I love to organize quite complex projects.
_____	I enjoy training other Christians.
_____	I don't mind tasks that others would rather not do.

Worksheet 9
(Instructions on page 185)

Worksheet: Developing Functional Structures

Step	Criterion:	Measurement:
_____	_____	_____
_____	_____	_____
_____	_____	_____
_____	_____	_____
_____	_____	_____
_____	_____	_____
_____	_____	_____
_____	_____	_____
_____	_____	_____
_____	_____	_____
_____	_____	_____
_____	_____	_____
_____	_____	_____
_____	_____	_____
_____	_____	_____

Worksheet: Evaluate your steps (Checklist 1)

Worksheet 10
(Instructions on page 189)

The following two checklists are designed to help you evaluate alternative approaches and discover the most biotic solution. The positive checklist on page 229 evaluates how well biotic principles have been integrated into a certain measure. The negative checklist on page 230 identifies those elements that ignore biotic principles. These lists give you a set of criteria to evaluate solutions which with some practice can be incorporated into the development of intended measures.

The positive checklist for the following measure:

This statement applies to the measure concerned:	Mostly Yes	Mostly No
1. Will it have long-term positive effects?	❑	❑
2. Will other areas of church life also be positively impacted?	❑	❑
3. Will it increase "production capacity"?	❑	❑
4. Has the possibility of multiplication been consciously built in?	❑	❑
5. Have the needs and gifts of those participating been recognized?	❑	❑
6. Is resistance dealt with constructively?	❑	❑
7. Does the intended goal have a positive impact on the original situation?	❑	❑
8. Does the measure support itself?	❑	❑
9. Do team members, activities, etc. complement each other?	❑	❑
10. Does this measure encourage variety in forms, styles, methods, etc.?	❑	❑
11. Does this measure integrate clear criteria for measuring success?	❑	❑
12. Has it been decided how and when the success of this step will be evaluated?	❑	❑

Worksheet: Evaluate your steps (Checklist 2)

Worksheet 11
(Instructions on page 189)

The negative checklist for the following measure:

_____

This statement applies to the measure concerned:	Mostly Yes	Mostly No
1. Is this an isolated island measure?	❏	❏
2. Is something here pushed through without consideration for long-term consequences?	❏	❏
3. Is the basis for this step the concern about a slow beginning?	❏	❏
4. Is the motto "Rather addition than no growth at all"?	❏	❏
5. Has there been an appeal to people's guilt?	❏	❏
6. Is resistance countered with appropriate counter force?	❏	❏
7. Is this measure a one-way measure?	❏	❏
8. Is it necessary to invest more energy because the measure ignores ways to "hit more than one fly with one swat"?	❏	❏
9. Is there a tendency to press everybody into the same mold?	❏	❏
10. Is there a feeling of competition between different workers, departments, etc.?	❏	❏
11. Are there other motives than church development driving this step?	❏	❏
12. Are "sacred cows" preserved rather than slaughtered?	❏	❏

Scoring:

The more often you have checked a " mostly yes" answer in the positive checklist and a "mostly no" in the negative checklist, the more biotic your measures. If you want to know exactly which biotic principle is being observed or ignored, you can use the following key. The questions in both checklists correspond to the following principles:

Questions 1/2: Interdependence
Questions 3/4: Multiplication
Questions 5/6: Energy transformation
Questions 7/8: Multi-usage
Questions 9/10: Symbiosis
Questions 11/12: Functionality

The Scientific Base of the Church Profile

The principles of natural church development have been developed on the basis of empirical studies of churches around the globe. But what is the scientific approach behind it? Since most pastors and church members who get involved in natural church development are not familiar with the methodical tools of the social sciences, here are some introductory remarks.

Why a scientific approach?

"You can mis-use a church as a guinea pig only for a limited time."

In the world today there is a great supply of models, recipes, theories and tips on the subject of church growth that sometimes even contradict each other. The more extended and international your search for information becomes, the more confusing is the spectrum of choices. Who knows what is what? What is right, what is wrong? And the most important question: Which of all these counsels are really applicable to the concrete situation of our church?

One thing is sure. A local church can only be misused as a guinea pig for a limited time. As time goes on, church development by trial and error leads to discontent and frustration, destroying even the best motivations of those involved in the ministry of the church.

For this reason, our institute is committed to study the factors of church growth scientifically and systematically. Our goal is to set new standards for church related research. Statements you find in our books will not reflect guesses based on "gut-level" feelings. We will only teach and pass along principles that can be proven to be universally valid.

The Goal of Our Research

During the last ten years our research has focused on two questions:

1. How can we develop a tool for church analysis that meets scientific criteria? Such a "church-test" is necessary to be able to decide which steps would make sense in the current situation of any church. Without accurate diagnosis, no appropriate therapy can be started.

The quality index indicates how well the quality of a church is developed. It is based on evaluating the eight quality characteristics of growing churches.

2. In light of scientific research, which recommendations for church growth are turning out to be possibly untenable or even counterproductive? What are the principles through which God builds his church?

In the meantime, our research of more than 1000 churches in 32 countries of the world has enabled us to find answers to both of these questions.

What does "scientific" mean?

In order to not perish in the jungle of well-meaning advice, it is important that we deal with the trustworthiness of the many resources for church development. One criterion for trustworthiness is the scientific basis of a given approach. Can it be proven empirically that in any specific situation, a certain measure will lead to a desired effect? Or is this merely the beautiful experience of a certain, possibly well-known church that sells the idea now to the rest of the Christian church as a cure-all?

"Can it be proven that in any specific situation, a certain measure will lead to a desired effect?"

When we use the term "science" we mean the tools of the social sciences. We are not talking here about research in the realm of the Arts and Sciences. As a spiritual reality, the "church" is an entity which is not only accessible to theology, but also to the social sciences.

What then are the criteria offered by science for measuring a process like the conducting of a church profile on a scientific basis?

How Scientific Statements Originate

The branch of science that deals with this area is called the test theory. It belongs to the realm of organizational-psychological diagnostics and focuses on examining the relationship between the answering of test questions (called "items"), and their dependency on the peculiarities of the respondents, on the characteristics of the items themselves, and on the situation in which the items are answered.

The quality index shows how well a quality is developed in a church. The index is based on an evaluation of the "eight quality characteristics."

See NCD, page 20

When an item in our survey reads, "Our church consciously promotes the multiplication of small groups through cell division," the degree of agreement to this statement depends not only on the actual small group multiplication taking place in the church; the clear wording of the question and the current situation also play a significant role. For example, any theoretical knowledge that multiplication would be a good thing can lead to wishful thinking and thus to an overrating of the situation.

Even though we are only interested in measuring the extent of the multiplication of small groups in a given church, we have to take into account the fact that each answer to our test question accumulates some error. The error that results in the situation in which the answer takes place is non-systematic and random. This has the advantage that, measured across several persons, the error cancels itself out.

Each Statement Contains Inaccuracies

How Accurate Is the Church Profile?

"It was important to develop a questionnaire that can measure the quality characteristics of a church, and accurately determine its minimum factor."

But what about errors caused by the questions themselves, that is, ambiguous questions that could be understood in different ways by different people or questions that ask about something that constantly changes? Here we are dealing with a quality criterion for tests that is called reliability, which has to do with the accuracy and trustworthiness of a test. If you repeat the test and get the same results (provided that nothing has changed, and that you are working with data from many people), then the test is reliable. If you get a different result, the difference between the two measurements is billed to the inaccuracy account of the test.

In the case of the church profile, this observation does not help us that much, because there is probably no church which would agree to become an unchangeable block of ice so that the reliability of the church profile can be tested. Yet even here the field of statistics has found ways to overcome these obstacles and offers some relatively complicated ways to calculate a test's reliability.

The Reliability of the Church Profile

The reliability of the church profile was examined in a study started at the University of Würzburg and continued by our institute. There were 201 participating churches. From these churches 211 pastors and 3,413 church members filled out the questionnaire we used at that time. After analyzing the data, revising the questionnaire, and analyzing the new data with a professional statistics program, it was possible to develop a new questionnaire that is able to measure the crucial quality characteristics of a church exactly and reliably, thus accurately determining its minimum factor.

(A note for professionals: The scales of the church profile have a reliability between $r = 0.75$ and $r = 0.89$ depending on the specific scale. For a test with an organizational diagnostic purpose, these are very high values.)

In the meantime, we have examined these results on 34,314 persons in 1188 churches in 32 countries.

What Is the Church Profile Actually Measuring?

A further quality criterion for a scientific test is validity. While relia-bility indicates how accurately a test is measuring something, it does not give any information about what is being measured, which is exactly the question validity deals with. In theory, it is possible that despite a high reliability score, a church profile actually measures something completely different from the quality characteristics of a church. For example, instead of measuring the ability of the pastor to empower his leaders, it might actually measure the level of sympathy towards the pastor on the part of the members.

"The correlation between growth and the eight quality characteristics is, statistically, highly significant."

The validity of the church profile was ensured in three ways:

1. To begin with, there was the question asking if the eight quality characteristics we use (see Part 3 in this book) really do exist or if they represent merely a mental model that exists only on paper. A prerequisite for validity is that the breakdown of a church's quali-ty into exactly eight characteristics does not only make sense the-oretically but is based on empirical evidence. By using a compli-cated mathematical procedure called "confirmatory factor analy-sis" you can test if the theoretically designed data structure can actually be found in the data. The result: The eight quality char-acteristics do not only make great sense on paper, they are also sci-entifically sound.

2. Validity also means that the test results must agree highly with a related external criterion. Thus an intelligence test, for instance, would be valid only if it indicates that students with good grades also have high intelligence scores, but students with bad grades have low intelligence scores. As external criterion, we selected the growth of the church. So we divided the churches participating in our survey into two extreme groups, "growing" churches and "declining" churches. The illustration on this page shows how large the difference actually was between growing and declining churches in all eight quali-ty areas (the normative average value of all churches studied was set as a mean score of 50 with a standard deviation of 15). The correlation between growth and the eight quality characteristics is therefore quite high (which in addition to our comparison of extreme groups, can also be proven mathematically precisely through the validity coefficient).

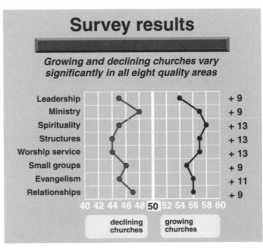

Survey results

Growing and declining churches vary significantly in all eight quality areas

Leadership	+ 9
Ministry	+ 9
Spirituality	+ 13
Structures	+ 13
Worship service	+ 13
Small groups	+ 9
Evangelism	+ 11
Relationships	+ 9

40 42 44 46 48 **50** 52 54 56 58 60

declining churches   growing churches

3. Each item on the questionnaire is assigned to one of the eight quality characteristics. "Empowering leadership" for instance, has fifteen items. One of them reads: "The members of the leadership of the church focus on assignments they are gifted for." Another reads: "There is a contagious optimism which emanates from the leaders of our church (pastor, church leadership, other leaders)." For "inspiring worship" one of nine items reads: "Attending our worship services is an inspiring experience for me." Let's suppose that (calculated over many churches) a high percentage of members, whenever they check that their pastor radiates with optimism, also check that he is ministering on the basis of his gifts. In contrast, whenever other members check that the pastor radiates little optimism they also do not feel he is operating within his gifts. In this case we speak of a positive relationship between the two items.

The Correlation Coefficient

This relationship that is statistically calculated from the answers of the respondents is the correlation coefficient. Through a value between $+1$ and -1, the coefficient expresses the direction of this relationship (positive or negative) and how strong it is. The greater the number of members who either agree or disagree at the same time with two statements, the more the coefficient approaches the value of $+1$. If most members characterize their pastor as pessimistic while finding the worship service inspiring, the coefficient will approach a value of -1. A correlation coefficient of zero or near zero means that there is no systematic relationship between the two items concerned.

If the test is to pass the validity test, all items that are associated with a certain quality characteristic have to show a strong, positive correlation. With items of the other quality characteristics, they must not have any, or only a very low, correlation. For our example, this would mean that the optimism of the pastor and his gift-orientation should usually be seen simultaneously positive or negative, while the level of inspiration of the worship service should be estimated independently, sometimes this way, sometimes another way.

A Measuring Instrument for Church Quality

Our analysis has shown that the questions assigned to a certain quality area have a high correlation among each other (up to $+0.82$) while the correlation to questions assigned to other quality characteristics is low. In practice this means that the items in our survey form are suited to identify the eight quality characteristics and to distinguish between them. With such a church profile it is, therefore, indeed possible to measure the quality of a church.

Other Exciting Products from ChurchSmart Resources

Natural Church Development

By Christian Schwarz

In an attempt to put denominational and cultural distinctives aside, the author has researched 1000 churches in 32 countries to determine the quality characteristics that growing, healthy churches share. Schwarz's research indicates that quality churches score high in eight quality characteristics, but will only grow to the level that their minimum factor (or lowest of these eight characteristics) will allow them. This book is a must read!

ChurchSmart price $19.95

Raising Leaders for the Harvest

By Robert Logan & Neil Cole

Raising Leaders for the Harvest introduces the concept of Leadership Farm Systems, an organic process of leadership development which results in natural and spontaneous multiplication of disciples, groups, ministries and churches. This resource kit includes six audio cassettes and an action planning guide with worksheets. Discover how to raise leaders in your church for the harvest in your community!

ChurchSmart price $60.00

Focused Living Resource Kit

By Terry Walling

Focused Living is a personal development process designed to help believers bring strategic focus to their life and ministry. Focus is obtained by examining their past (Perspective — Personal Time-Line), clarifying their future (Focus — Personal Mission Statement) and identifying resources that will facilitate future growth and effectiveness (Mentoring — Personal Mentors). This resource includes six audio cassettes, three self-discovery workbooks and a leader's guide.

ChurchSmart price $60.00